Honey Tree Publishing
www.honeytreepublishingus.com

Copyright © 2025 by DJ Carroll
ISBN: 979-8-9986149-0-3
First Edition

The Hunter Head Game:
The Old World Rewarded Obedience.
The New World Demands Killer Instincts.

All rights reserved. No part of this publication may be reproduced, stored in a retrieval system, or transmitted in any form or by any means—electronic, mechanical, photocopying, recording, or otherwise—without the prior written permission of the copyright holder, except in the case of brief quotations used in reviews or scholarly works. This book is a work of original authorship. Generative Artificial Intelligence tools assisted in developing this publication, including support in brainstorming, drafting, editing, and formatting.

For permissions, inquiries, or more information, please contact:
DJ Carroll at dj@coachcarroll.com

TheHunterHeadGame.com

Coach Carroll., 1988 -The Hunter Head Game.

1. Business. 2. Self-Help 3. Motivational. 4. Trade.

Edited by Dr. Tytianna Ringstaff

Cover Art by Andrew Stearman andy@carroll.media

Printed in the United States of America

# Dedication

For the ones who feel it in their gut but haven't jumped yet.

The ones staring down the safe path… and starting to hate it.

For the ones who leapt—

and now wake up every day fighting to turn chaos into something real.

And for the ones who've been at it a while,

who've lost the fire, the edge,

the killer instinct that once made them dangerous.

This book is for all of you.

The ones who were never built to stay the same.

It's time to move out of your bullshit, and into your potential.

**Attention Amazon Buyers:**

Be sure to register at www.hunterheadgame.com to receive your resources and bonuses.

# Acknowledgements

Writing this book was a battle—and I didn't fight it alone.

To my wife, Victoria—your love, patience, and belief in me were the fuel behind every late night and early morning. I'm building this legacy for us and for our children.

To my family—especially my brother Nick—you've always had my back, in business and in life.

To my dad who taught me how to hustle.

To my mom who always encouraged me to dream bigger.

To my grandma who taught me the art of poetry.

To my teams—your support was more than appreciated—it was required!

To my readers, clients, and those who've followed this journey—thank you!

And to every teacher, hater, or doubter who prophesied my downfall:

**You helped sharpen me.**

## Table of Contents

**PROLOGUE** | The Hunter's Utopia — 1

**CHAPTER 1** | Unleashing the Hunter Within — 15

**CHAPTER 2** | Marking Your Target — 33

**CHAPTER 3** | Growl and Grit — 57

**CHAPTER 4** | Kill Season — 99

**CHAPTER 5** | Stacking Skulls — 137

**CHAPTER 6** | Carnivore Camaraderie — 157

**CHAPTER 7** | The Wild Fights Back — 177

**CHAPTER 8** | From Prey to Predator — 219

**CHAPTER 9** | Life as a Hunter — 231

**CHAPTER 10** | Ascending to Apex — 241

**EPILOGUE** | Licking Your Lips — 246

**The Apex Hunter**: Battle Plan — 251

**References** — 253

# PROLOGUE

# The Hunter's Utopia

And so it was, there were those who wandered, seeking, yet never finding. They were fed, yet always hungry. They toiled, yet never conquered. Their hands grasped, but their hearts were empty, for they knew not the way of the hunter.

But among them rose a different kind. One whose eyes saw beyond the horizon, whose hunger was not for survival alone, but for dominion. This one did not wait for the harvest— he pursued the kill. He did not ask for permission— he carved his own path through the wilderness of mediocrity.

To the lost, this book is a riddle. To the weak, it is a burden. To the meek, it is a storm. But to the hunter, it is a map, a weapon, and a prophecy. If you stand at the threshold of greatness, uncertain of your place, let this be the fire that awakens you. If you have tasted success yet still crave more, let this be the blade that sharpens your edge.

For the hunter is not born, but forged. This is the domain of those who refuse the comfort of the herd, who take ownership of their fate. It is the kingdom of those who know that fear is a shadow, that patience is a virtue, but urgency is a weapon.

And so it was that I, too, was hunted. There was a time when I built, only to watch it burn— a time when I rose, only to be struck down. But a hunter does not stay grounded. He does not mourn the loss. He sharpens his blade. He learns, and he waits— until the moment comes to take back what is his. What lies ahead is not comfort, not ease, but power— power that belongs to those who will claim it.

*And so, I ask you, wanderer at the edge of this fire: Are you here to be fed, or are you here to hunt?*

## Identifying If This Book is for You

This book is for individuals who want to take ownership of their lives and circumstances. If you're reading these words, chances are you're searching for something more – a way to break free from the constraints that have held you back, a path to transformation that empowers rather than diminishes your potential.

This book is for the person who wants to be the aggressor, not the victim. There are two fundamental roles in nature: the hunter and the hunted. In business and life, this same dynamic plays out daily. Some people actively pursue opportunities, challenges, and growth, while others remain passive, reactive, and ultimately at the mercy of their environment.

You may recognize yourself as someone who:

- Has grown tired of being at the mercy of external circumstances

- Feels the untapped potential within you despite facing obstacles

- Identifies as an underdog but knows you're capable of more

- Desires to break free from traditional employment constraints

- Seeks to outperform your competition rather than merely keeping pace

- Wants to transform your approach to business challenges

From hunted to hunter is the ultimate transformation anyone can make in this world. It represents the shift from reacting to acting, surviving to thriving, from being defined by circumstances to defining your own path forward.

If you've picked up this book, you're already showing the instincts of a hunter. You're seeking knowledge, strategies, and mindsets to give you an edge. You realize success is not accidental. It's pursued with intention, strategy, and relentless determination.

This book will not offer easy shortcuts or overnight solutions. However, it will provide a framework for thinking, acting, and persisting like the most successful entrepreneurs in today's competitive landscape. It will challenge you to develop the hunter mentality that separates those who merely dream from those who achieve.

If you're ready to stop being prey and start being the predator in your market, this book was written for you.

## Defining the Entrepreneurial Hunter

What exactly is an entrepreneurial hunter? Throughout this book, we must clearly distinguish between a hunter's mentality and a hunted mentality. This differentiation is fundamental to understanding the transformation I invite you to make.

Entrepreneurial hunters are not defined merely by their profession or business card title. Rather, it's a mindset, an approach to challenges, and a way of moving through the business world that sets them apart from the masses.

An entrepreneurial hunter:

## Takes Ownership

Hunters don't make excuses – they make decisions. When faced with obstacles, they don't say, "I can't because..." Instead, they ask, "How can I?" They understand that owning their circumstances, regardless of how unfair or challenging, is the first step toward changing them. The hunter recognizes that while we can't control everything that happens to us, we absolutely control our response.

## Operates Strategically

A hunter doesn't wander, hoping to stumble upon success. They study the terrain, understand their prey, and develop a strategic approach that maximizes their chances of success. In business, this means analyzing markets, understanding customer needs, and positioning yourself advantageously against competitors.

## Acts With Urgency

While the hunted react only when threatened, hunters move with purpose and initiative. They don't wait for perfect conditions or absolute certainty – they assess risks intelligently and take decisive action. The entrepreneurial hunter understands that in business, hesitation often means missed opportunities.

## Shows Resilience

Every hunt includes setbacks – missed shots, lost trails, and unexpected complications. A hunter's response to failure ultimately defines them rather than the absence of failure. The entrepreneurial hunter views failures as data points and learning opportunities rather than permanent defeats. They lick their wounds briefly, then get back on the trail.

## Develops Their Skills

Hunters are constantly honing their abilities. They practice their aim, improve their tracking, and learn from each experience. The entrepreneurial hunter invests in their development, understanding that their capabilities directly impact their success. They read, learn, train, and apply new knowledge consistently.

## Embraces Discomfort

The hunted seek comfort and safety above all else. Hunters understand that growth happens at the edge of comfort. They willingly endure temporary discomfort – early mornings, rejection, uncertainty, risk – in pursuit of their objectives. This willingness to be uncomfortable sets them apart in a world that increasingly prioritizes ease over achievement.

## Builds Strategic Alliances

Even lone wolves understand the value of the pack when taking down larger prey. Entrepreneurial hunters build relationships with others who complement their skills and share their drive. They know the right connections can multiply their effectiveness and open doors to bigger opportunities.

The entrepreneurial hunter isn't born, but forged through conscious choice and consistent action. Throughout history, some of the most successful entrepreneurs came from humble beginnings but adopted the hunter mindset that ultimately transformed their circumstances.

In today's business landscape, with its rapidly changing technologies, shifting consumer behaviors, and global competition, the hunter mindset is more valuable than ever. Those who can spot opportunities, move decisively, adapt quickly, and persist through challenges will thrive where others merely survive.

As we progress through this book, you'll learn how to develop and strengthen these hunter characteristics within yourself, regardless of your starting point. The transformation from hunted to hunter begins with understanding what you're aiming to become.

## Fear, Ownership, and the Mindset Shift

The transformation from hunted to hunter requires confronting the most significant obstacle most of us face: fear. In my years of working with entrepreneurs and building my own businesses, I've observed that the number one fear holding people back isn't failure. It's the fear of other people's opinions.

This fear is powerful enough to keep talented, capable individuals trapped in lives that don't fulfill them. When you worry constantly about how others will judge your choices, you make decisions based on external validation rather than internal conviction. And as any hunter knows, that path leads to going hungry.

I learned this lesson early in my journey. As a young man in high school with entrepreneurial ambitions, I found myself sitting across from my guidance counselor and chemistry teacher as they earnestly tried to talk me out of starting my first business. What they didn't know was that I had already launched it. I was simply deciding whether to forgo college to pursue my entrepreneurial endeavors full-time.

They painted a stark picture: I would never be as successful as a businessman as if I went to school and became a chemical engineer. The certainty in their voices was almost convincing. After all, they were the experts, the authorities, the ones who supposedly knew better than an ambitious young man with dreams bigger than his résumé.

But something in me recognized that this was a pivotal moment – a choice between living by others' expectations or charting my own course. It was the first of many times I would have to decide: hunter or hunted?

Ownership is critical. In the entrepreneurial context, ownership extends far beyond just having your name on a business license. It means taking complete responsibility for everything: every decision you make, every mistake, and every problem that arises. There's no passing the buck, no blaming circumstances, no hiding behind excuses.

As Jocko Willink explains in his book "Extreme Ownership" (2015), true leaders don't deflect when things go wrong – they absorb responsibility. They don't say, "My team failed me" or "The market conditions were unfavorable." Instead, they ask, "How did I fail to prepare my team?" or "How did I misread the market?"

I operated from the understanding that if I decided not to go to college – potentially disappointing my parents, teachers, and friends – I would ultimately have to own how it all turned out. There would be no one else to blame if things went south.

Fortunately, things didn't turn out badly. Today, I have a beautiful family, a wife and children who love me, and an income that allows me to care for my immediate and extended family while giving back to charities and causes close to my heart. But these benefits, this upside, came directly from taking full ownership of my path.

The mindset shift from hunted to hunter happens when you stop asking, "Why is this happening to me?" and ask, "What can I do about it?" It occurs when you move from a position of reaction to a position of initiative. It manifests when you quit blaming external factors for your circumstances and instead view those circumstances as the playing field on which you operate – not as excuses for inaction.

This shift isn't easy. It requires confronting uncomfortable truths about yourself and taking responsibility even when it would be easier to point fingers. It means accepting that while you can't control everything that happens in the business world, you absolutely control your response to those events.

The hunted say: "I can't because..." The hunter asks: "How can I?"

The hunted think: "Someone should solve this problem."

The hunter thinks: "I'll solve this problem and create value."

The hunted waits for permission.

The hunter seeks forgiveness rather than permission.

This mindset shift doesn't happen overnight. It's cultivated through daily choices, repeatedly choosing responsibility over blame, action over complaint, and ownership over victimhood. But once this shift begins to take hold, everything changes - not just in your business, but in how you view every challenge and opportunity life presents.

## The Power of Urgency vs. Patience

One of the most critical balancing acts for any entrepreneurial hunter is knowing when to strike quickly and when to wait strategically. This tension between urgency and patience defines much of the entrepreneurial journey, and mastering it can mean the difference between sustained success and spectacular failure.

When I started my first business at 18, it was all hustle and grind - a constant state of urgency. Go, go, go. Keep your head above water. And truthfully, there's a period where this approach is necessary to gain momentum. The most successful entrepreneurs I know all share stories of those early days fueled by caffeine, determination, and a relentless drive to make things happen *now*.

However, as I've grown, hired better coaches, and matured over the past 18 years, I've come to appreciate that having a solid strategic plan allows you to develop patience. The hunter who understands the seasonal patterns of their prey doesn't waste energy chasing when conditions aren't right. Similarly, the wise entrepreneur learns that building something meaningful takes time.

Gary Vaynerchuk captures this perfectly with his philosophy of "macro patience, micro speed," which is the hunter's paradox: moving with intensity and urgency in your daily actions while maintaining the strategic patience to see your larger vision unfold over the years.

I believe anything is possible with a long enough time horizon. The challenge is that most people underestimate what they can accomplish in 5, 7, or 10 years while simultaneously overestimating what they can achieve in the next seven days. This misalignment of expectations leads to both short-term frustration and long-term underachievement.

The cost of misaligning urgency and patience can be devastating. Consider Theranos, where Elizabeth Holmes moved with such urgency to make her vision a reality that she promised investors technology that hadn't yet been developed. This rush to market without the patience to perfect the underlying science led to one of the most spectacular business collapses in recent history.

Conversely, slow movement can be just as fatal. Look at once-dominant companies like Yahoo and AOL, which failed to adapt quickly to changing market conditions. In 2000, at its peak, Yahoo had a market capitalization of $125 billion. By the time Verizon acquired it in 2017, it was valued at just $4.48

billion – a staggering 96% decline. Their patience became complacency, and the markets punished them accordingly.

In today's business environment, where technology accelerates change and social media creates unprecedented distractions, finding this balance is more challenging than ever. It's easy to waste hours scrolling through feeds, caught in what appears urgent but is merely noise. I don't believe we've fully grasped the effect of social media addiction and constant connection – much like society once saw no problem with people smoking cigarettes on airplanes.

So, how do you determine when to act with urgency versus when to exercise patience? I've learned to filter everything through my strategic plan. When a new idea emerges – and God knows I come up with a million new ideas every day, just like most entrepreneurs – I ask: Does this map back to the overall strategic plan? Is this aligned with where we're ultimately trying to go?

You must start with the end in mind, visualize your destination, and then work backward. If the idea, activity, meeting, phone call, or even text message doesn't connect to that strategy, it probably doesn't deserve the same urgency as the other priorities on your list.

The disciplined hunter doesn't chase every movement in the underbrush. They discern between the rustling of their prey and the background noise of the forest. Similarly, the successful entrepreneur develops the wisdom to act with appropriate speed on the right opportunities while allowing less critical matters to wait.

This balance isn't static – it shifts with your business's stage, market conditions, and personal capacity. The key is developing the discernment to know which mode serves you best in each situation. When you master this, you'll find yourself moving with purpose rather than merely reacting to the latest crisis or opportunity.

## Personal Story: Rising Above Adversity

My journey from hunted to hunter began with Yard Smart Lawn Care and Landscaping, my first business, which I started at eighteen. I launched with just $300 – $100 saved from working at a local gas station and $100 each borrowed from my mom and grandmother. That modest sum allowed me to buy my first push mower and put a down payment on a 1989 Ford F-150 – shit brown and terrible on gas mileage, but it was my ticket to independence.

I had all the cards stacked against me: minimal capital, no business experience, and perhaps most challenging, no support from my teachers or guidance counselor. I felt the weight of disappointing my parents by turning down football scholarship offers and choosing not to be the first in my family to attend college.

In my working-class, blue-collar family, the opportunity to attend college on a scholarship was something most would have celebrated without question. But I recognized even then that following that expected path would likely leave me as just another broke kid with a degree. And if there was one thing I was sure about, I was tired of being poor.

I remember vividly a childhood moment that crystallized this feeling. I wanted to watch WWE WrestleMania on pay-per-view – a $20 expense that felt monumental at the time. When I asked my dad if we could get it, he said we couldn't afford it. Frustrated, I shouted, "I hate being poor!" and stomped to my room.

My dad followed me and delivered a lesson I've never forgotten. He showed me what being genuinely poor meant for the next couple of weeks – no TV, bicycle, or snacks after school. It was a harsh but practical lesson in perspective and gratitude for what we did have.

I understand now why my father took that approach. He had risen from truly desperate circumstances. Recently, he sent me a newspaper clipping that chronicled a defining moment from his childhood. The headline read: "Mother jailed, 11 children taken to home." It detailed how my grandmother was jailed on disorderly conduct charges while nine of her eleven children, including my father, were taken to a children's home after being found in an unheated three-room house, with barely any food, dirty clothing, and mostly without shoes.

My father, who emerged from those circumstances, worked tirelessly to provide for me, my brother, and my mom. His relentless work ethic flows in my blood and has shaped my approach to challenges. From him, I learned that adversity isn't just something to endure – it's something that, when faced head-on, becomes an asset, giving you both a chip on your shoulder and a depth of resilience that others may never develop.

Starting that lawn care business wasn't just about making money. I declared that I wouldn't be defined by circumstances or limited by others' expectations. But that decision came with unexpected social costs.

I remember the first day I wore one of my lawn care shirts to school – a shirt I had made myself with iron-on transfer paper printed from my computer. I was so proud of it, with "Yard Smart Lawn Care and Landscaping" displayed across my chest. But when I got to school, people laughed and picked on me because I wore work boots and a neon green safety-colored shirt instead of Abercrombie, Hollister, or the newest pair of Nikes.

Even though my mom made sure my brother and I both got a new pair of shoes every year at the start of school, I chose to wear my boots because I knew as soon as the bell rang, I'd be out hustling, cutting the yards I'd worked so hard to schedule. Feeling embarrassed and mocked, I can see how that would've been an easy place to say, "You know what, maybe this isn't for me. Maybe I should just go to school and be like everyone else."

But that moment of social rejection became another turning point where I chose the hunter's path. Every lawn I mowed, and every customer I acquired was proof that the hunter mentality could overcome obstacles that seem insurmountable when viewed through the lens of the hunted.

The business grew, not overnight, but steadily through consistent effort and applying principles I'll share throughout this book. Each small victory built confidence. Each setback provided valuable lessons. And gradually, the hunter instincts in all of us are sharpened through practical application.

As you read this, I know you have your own story, too. You can think of a time when you were down, when something terribly challenging happened, and you had to rise above it. That, my friend, is part of the journey. Those experiences of overcoming adversity aren't liabilities – they're assets that have made you stronger than you might realize.

The path of the hunter isn't about avoiding difficulties or having an easy start. It's about transforming those difficulties into fuel that propels you forward. It's about recognizing that your background, whatever it may be, has equipped you with unique perspectives and strengths that others may not possess.

As you move through this book, I invite you to reconsider any adversity you've faced not as evidence that you can't succeed, but as preparation for the success that awaits the hunter who refuses to be defined as prey.

# CHAPTER 1

# Unleashing the Hunter Within

*Two spirits dwell in the heart of every person—one gazes toward distant horizons, while the other stares at the ground beneath its feet. One shapes destiny; the other is shaped by it.*

*Across the tapestry of time, many have wandered with empty hands outstretched, forever waiting. They speak of fate as though invisible hands have already written tomorrow's story. Their wisdom rings hollow; wisdom without action is like a blade that never cuts, a fire that gives no warmth. Yet among the waiting masses walk the few who move with purpose. They see beyond what is, to what could be. The world before them is not fixed but fluid, not rigid but malleable to their touch. They forge paths where others see only wilderness.*

*Gaze now into the mirror of your soul. What eyes look back at you? Those that seek permission? Or those that need none?*

*When darkness threatens, the hunted whispers, "What if I fail?"*

*The hunter smiles and asks, "What if I triumph?"*

*The ancient pattern reveals itself: Neither the strongest nor the swiftest claim the prize, but those who recognize treasure while others see only stone stake their claim while others hesitate in doubt.*

*Standing at the crossroads of decision, which path calls to you? The worn trail leading to comfortable shadows? Or the unmarked way, where each step breaks new ground?*

*And so, the hunter rises, not because the path is clear, but because the hunger is greater than the fear.*

# The Hunter's Mentality vs. The Hunted

In nature, the distinction between predator and prey is unambiguous. The gazelle runs; the lion pursues. The rabbit hides; the hawk soars overhead, searching. This primal dynamic has shaped the evolution of species for millions of years. Though we've built cities and technologies that distance us from our wild origins, this fundamental dichotomy remains in our psychology.

In the modern business world, this dynamic plays out every day, not in the savannas or forests, but in marketplaces, board rooms, and entrepreneurial ventures. Some individuals instinctively position themselves as hunters—active, strategic, and purposeful in pursuing opportunities. Others, often unconsciously, adopt the mindset of the hunted—reactive, defensive, and defined by the circumstances around them rather than by their vision.

The difference between these two mentalities is not merely philosophical—it manifests in tangible outcomes and lived experiences. Let me illustrate this contrast:

## The Hunted Mentality:

The hunted individual lives in a constant state of reaction. They respond to market changes only when forced to, adapt to new technologies only when their hand is called, and pursue new opportunities only when their current situation becomes untenable. They are:

- Driven by fear rather than ambition, making decisions to avoid negative outcomes rather than to create positive ones

- Focused on security above all else, often sacrificing growth and fulfillment for the illusion of stability

- Perpetually explaining why things happened *to* them, externalizing both blame and control

- Waiting for permission or validation before taking action

- Defining success defensively as "not failing" rather than affirmatively as achieving specific objectives

The hunted wake up wondering what challenges the day will bring and how they'll respond. They view competitors as threats to avoid rather than as worthy adversaries who sharpen their skills. They see market changes as disruptions rather than opportunities.

## The Hunter Mentality:

In stark contrast, the hunter approaches the business landscape with intentionality and purpose. They:

- Proactively seek opportunities rather than waiting for them to appear

- Take calculated risks after assessing both potential rewards and dangers

- Own their circumstances completely, never deflecting responsibility for outcomes

- Act decisively once they've gathered sufficient (but rarely complete) information

- Define success offensively in terms of specific objectives achieved, territories conquered, and value created

The hunter wakes up planning which opportunities to pursue and how to overcome the obstacles. They view competitors as part of the ecosystem that makes them stronger and sharper. They see market changes as chances to gain an advantage and create new value.

This distinction goes beyond simple optimism versus pessimism. A hunter isn't merely positive—they're strategic. They don't deny challenges or risks; they acknowledge them clearly and develop plans to address them. The hunted aren't necessarily negative—they're reactive, allowing external circumstances to dictate their responses rather than charting their own course.

Consider how these mentalities might approach a typical business scenario: a new competitor enters the market with an innovative offering that threatens to disrupt existing business models.

The hunted responds with fear and defensiveness: "This will hurt our business. We need to protect what we have. Maybe we should lower prices to keep our customers."

The hunter responds with strategic aggression: "This new entrant has identified something customers want that the market wasn't providing. What can we learn from this? How might we adapt our offering to provide even greater value? Where are they vulnerable, and how can we outperform them where it matters most to customers?"

The difference isn't just semantic—it leads to entirely different strategic responses and, ultimately, different outcomes.

The question becomes: where do you fall on this spectrum? Few people are pure hunters or pure prey in every situation. Most of us adopt different postures in different contexts. You might be a hunter in your professional life but hunted in your personal relationships. You might be a hunter when pursuing clients but hunted when dealing with regulators or investors.

The first step toward developing a consistent hunter mentality is honest self-assessment. Consider these questions:

- When faced with challenges, is your first instinct to explain why they're happening or to develop a plan to overcome them?

- Do you spend more time thinking about what might go wrong or the opportunities you want to pursue?

- When you succeed, do you attribute that success primarily to your efforts and decisions or favorable circumstances?

- When you fail, do you look at what you could have done differently, or at external factors contributing to the outcome?

- Do you act only when you feel confident of success, or are you willing to move forward with imperfect information?

There are no "right" answers to these questions in the abstract. The point isn't to judge yourself but to understand your default patterns. The hunter mentality isn't something you're born with or without—it's a set of habits and perspectives developed through conscious practice.

Throughout my career, I've watched individuals transform from hunted to hunter. I've seen formerly reactive managers become proactive leaders. I've witnessed risk-averse employees become bold entrepreneurs. I've observed defensive business owners become aggressive market-makers. The common thread in each transformation was the decision—

made repeatedly, day after day—to think and act like a hunter rather than like prey.

This transformation begins with a simple but profound shift: taking complete ownership of your circumstances and results, not just the good ones. This doesn't mean blaming yourself when things outside your control go wrong. It means asking, "What could I have done differently?" rather than "Why did this happen to me?"

In the coming sections, we'll explore how to identify your unique strengths as a hunter and how to leverage the power of ownership to transform not just your mindset but your results. For now, I invite you to consider the following: In which areas of your business and life are you already operating as a hunter? And in which areas have you been adopting the posture of the hunted?

## Understanding Your Strengths & Skills

Every hunter in the natural world has evolved specific advantages—the falcon has keen eyesight, the wolf has stamina and pack coordination, and the lion has raw power and stealth. Similarly, as an entrepreneurial hunter, your success depends on identifying and leveraging your unique strengths while developing the essential skills all hunters must possess.

In my experience working with entrepreneurs across various industries, I've observed that many struggle not because they lack ability, but because they're hunting with the wrong weapons. They're trying to succeed using skills that don't align with their natural strengths.

The first step to becoming an effective hunter is honest self-assessment. You need to know what you're naturally good at, what energizes you, and where you have room to grow. It's not about ego or false modesty. It's about pragmatic self-knowledge that allows you to position yourself for maximum effectiveness.

Look back at the times when you've been most successful—whether in business, academics, sports, relationships, or any other domain. What patterns emerge? Were you leveraging analytical thinking? Creative problem-solving? Relationship-building? Strategic planning? Tactical execution? The activities that have historically led to your greatest successes often reveal your innate strengths.

Similarly, consider what activities drain you versus what energizes you. True strengths aren't just things you're good at—they're capabilities that invigorate you when you use them. If you find yourself exhausted after certain types of work, even if you perform adequately, that signals that you're operating outside your zone of natural strength.

As you identify your strengths, remember that the goal isn't to ignore your weaknesses entirely. Instead, it's to build your business strategy around your strengths while either developing your weak areas to an acceptable level or finding ways to complement them through partnerships, team members, or systems.

From my observation, successful entrepreneurial hunters typically possess a combination of the following core skills:

## Strategic Vision

Hunters don't just respond to what's directly in front of them—they scan the horizon, assess the terrain, and develop a plan before taking action. They see beyond immediate opportunities to identify larger patterns and possibilities in business. It's about asking, "Where is this market heading?" rather than "How can I make a sale today?"

I've found that strategic vision isn't just about being smart—it's about being willing to regularly step back from the day-to-day operations to consider the bigger picture. It's about studying your industry, competitors, and adjacent markets to spot trends and opportunities before others.

## Decisive Action

While the hunted hesitate, the hunter moves with purpose. Analysis paralysis is the enemy of entrepreneurial success. You'll never have perfect information, and waiting until you do means missing opportunities, which doesn't mean being reckless. It means becoming comfortable making decisions with 70-80% of the ideal information understanding that speed often trumps perfection in competitive environments. The most successful entrepreneurs I know have developed a bias toward action, recognizing that an imperfect decision executed quickly is usually better than a perfect decision that comes too late.

## Resilient Persistence

Every hunt includes setbacks, false starts, and missed opportunities. What separates successful entrepreneurs isn't an absence of failure but the ability to persevere through it.

Resilience isn't just about enduring hardship—it's about maintaining effectiveness despite challenges. It's about getting knocked down seven times and getting up eight. It's about viewing obstacles not as reasons to quit but as problems to solve.

I've watched countless talented entrepreneurs fail not because their ideas were flawed or their skills were insufficient but because they gave up when faced with the inevitable challenges of building something meaningful. The hunters who succeed are those who develop the mental toughness to keep moving forward when others retreat.

## Adaptive Learning

The business landscape constantly changes, with new technologies, competitors, and consumer preferences emerging regularly. The entrepreneurial hunter must be a perpetual learner, continually sharpening their skills and acquiring new ones. Reading voraciously, seeking feedback aggressively, studying both successes and failures in your field, and being willing to experiment with new approaches means developing a growth mindset that views challenges as opportunities to improve rather than as threats to your identity or capabilities.

## Relational Intelligence

Even lone wolves understand the importance of the pack when taking down larger prey. No entrepreneur succeeds entirely alone. Your ability to build relationships with customers, team members, investors, suppliers, and strategic partners will often determine your ultimate success.

This doesn't mean you need to be an extrovert—many successful entrepreneurs aren't—but it does mean developing the ability to understand others' perspectives, communicate effectively, build trust, and create mutually beneficial arrangements.

I've seen technically brilliant entrepreneurs fail because they couldn't build the relationships necessary to attract talent, secure funding, or retain customers. Conversely, I've watched entrepreneurs with modest technical skills build thriving businesses through their ability to connect with and influence others.

As you assess your own strengths and skills, be honest about where you excel naturally and where you need development. If you're strong in strategic vision but weak in decisive action, acknowledge this gap and work to close it. If you're naturally decisive but struggle with relational intelligence, find ways to complement this through team members or personal growth.

Remember, the goal isn't to become equally strong in all areas—that's neither realistic nor necessary. Rather, it's to leverage your natural advantages while ensuring you're not fatally weak in any essential area.

In my own journey, I recognized early that my strengths lay in spotting opportunities and taking decisive action. I could see possibilities others missed and wasn't afraid to move quickly to capitalize on them. However, I initially struggled with the discipline required for systematic execution over long periods. Recognizing this pattern allowed me to build structures and teams that complemented my natural strengths while shoring up my areas of weakness.

Your journey from hunted to hunter begins with this kind of clear-eyed self-assessment. Know your weapons, understand your hunting style, and build your strategy accordingly. In the next section, we'll explore how taking complete ownership of your circumstances—both challenges and opportunities—accelerates your transformation into an entrepreneurial hunter.

# The Role of Ownership in Entrepreneurship

If there's one concept that defines the hunter mentality more than any other, it's ownership. Not just ownership of a business—though that's often part of the journey—but ownership of your choices, circumstances, failures, and successes.

In the entrepreneurial context, ownership extends far beyond just having your name on a business license. It means taking complete responsibility for everything: every decision you make, every mistake, and every problem that arises. There's no passing the buck, no blaming circumstances, no hiding behind excuses.

As Jocko Willink explains in his book "Extreme Ownership," true leaders don't deflect when things go wrong – they absorb responsibility. They don't say, "My team failed me" or "The market conditions were unfavorable." Instead, they ask, "How did I fail to prepare my team?" or "How did I misread the market?"

I operated from the understanding that if I decided not to go to college – potentially disappointing my parents, teachers, and friends – I would ultimately have to own how it all turned out. There would be no one to blame if things went south.

The hunted mindset seeks someone or something to blame when faced with obstacles: the economy, the competition, unfair advantages others might have, lack of support, or insufficient resources. The hunter mindset asks, "Given these circumstances, how can I move forward?"

This distinction is crucial. When you blame external factors for your situation, you implicitly declare yourself powerless to change it. When you take ownership, you reclaim your agency and power to affect outcomes.

I've mentored many aspiring entrepreneurs over the years and observed that those who struggle most often can't or won't take full ownership of their circumstances. They constantly seek validation, permission, or guarantees before taking action. They want someone to tell them their idea will succeed before they commit to it. They want assurance that their investment of time and resources will pay off.

But here's the hard truth: entrepreneurship offers no such guarantees. The only certainty is that nothing will happen if you don't take ownership and action. The hunter doesn't wait for perfect conditions or absolute certainty – they assess risks intelligently and take decisive action.

Taking ownership isn't just about accepting blame when things go wrong. It's about recognizing that you are the primary agent in your own success story. It's about understanding that while you can't control everything that happens in the business world, you absolutely control your response to those events.

Consider how differently the hunted and the hunter approach a common business challenge: a major client decides not to renew their contract.

The hunted response might sound like: "This client was unreasonable. Their new procurement person never liked our company. The economy is forcing everyone to downsize. We're victims of circumstances beyond our control."

The hunter response would be more like: "We failed to demonstrate sufficient value to retain this client. We didn't adequately anticipate their evolving needs. We must examine what we could have done differently, learn from this experience, and develop a plan to replace this revenue while strengthening our relationships with existing clients."

Notice the difference? The hunted explanation absolves the entrepreneur of responsibility while simultaneously disempowering them. The hunter's explanation acknowledges reality, takes ownership, and focuses on actionable next steps.

This ownership mindset extends to every aspect of your business:

## Financial Results

If your profits aren't where you want them to be, the hunter doesn't blame the market, the economy, or competitors. They ask: "How can I create more value for customers? How can I communicate that value more effectively? How can I deliver that value more efficiently?"

## Team Performance

If your team isn't performing as needed, the hunter doesn't blame the talent pool, generational differences, or unreasonable expectations. They ask: "How am I failing to lead effectively? How can I better select, train, motivate, or resource my team? What systems or structures am I missing that would enable better performance?"

## Customer Satisfaction

If customers are unhappy or leaving, the hunter doesn't blame them for being difficult or unreasonable. They ask: "How are we failing to meet expectations? What promises are we making that we're not keeping? How can we better understand and address our customers' needs?"

## Personal Productivity

If you're not accomplishing what you intend to, the hunter doesn't blame interruptions, distractions, or lack of time. They ask: "How am I failing to manage my attention and energy? What systems do I need to put in place to ensure I focus on high-value activities? What am I saying yes to that I should be saying no to?"

This ownership mindset is both demanding and liberating. It's demanding because it places the responsibility for outcomes squarely on your shoulders. It's liberating because it puts you in the driver's seat of your entrepreneurial journey rather than leaving you at the mercy of external forces.

I remember clearly when this lesson crystallized for me. Early in my lawn care business, I lost several clients in a month. My initial reaction was to blame external factors—clients who didn't appreciate quality, competitors who undercut my prices, and homeowners who decided to mow their own lawns to save money.

But after a few days of frustration, I realized that this explanation, while comforting my ego, wasn't helping me solve the problem. I forced myself to take ownership: What value was I failing to deliver? How was I failing to communicate that value? What could I do differently to retain existing clients and replace the ones I'd lost?

This shift in perspective led to concrete actions—improving my service quality, communicating more regularly with clients about my work, offering additional services that added more value, and targeting a slightly different customer segment. Within two months, I had replaced the lost clients and was growing again.

The lesson was clear: taking ownership didn't make the problem my fault, but my responsibility was to solve it. And that made all the difference.

As you assess your mindset, ask yourself honestly: What's your first reaction when things don't go as planned in your business? Do you seek explanations or excuses? Do you focus on what you can't control or what you can? Do you see problems as obstacles placed in your path or as challenges you get to solve?

The hunter's path begins with ownership. It's not always comfortable and rarely easy, but it's the only path leading to the freedom and success most entrepreneurs seek.

The next chapter will explore translating this ownership mindset into a clear vision and strategic plan to guide your entrepreneurial hunt.

# CHAPTER 2

# Marking Your Target: Vision, Goals, and Performance

*In the beginning, the vision of the hunter was the hunt itself. The foolish hunter chases what appears before him, while the wise hunter first captures his prey in spirit before setting foot upon the sacred path.*

*Behold, three powers are bestowed upon those destined to rise: sight that pierces the veil of present circumstance, wisdom to chart the unseen path, and the will of iron that transforms divine thought into earthly conquest.*

*The eye blinded by immediate need claims only what lies at its feet. The mind without design circles like vultures above barren land. The spirit without purpose knows the weight of toil but never the glory of triumph.*

*Verily, before the arrow leaves the bow, before the spear pierces flesh, before the trap ensnares—the hunt is already written in the stars of the hunter's making.*

*Choose now thy path: Will you wander as chaff blown by the winds of chance, or will you ascend as the eagle who surveys all, strikes with purpose, and returns to the high places carrying that which was destined to be claimed?*

# The Importance of Visualization Before the Hunt

Every successful hunt begins before the hunter leaves their camp. The hunter studies the terrain, understands the habits of their prey, anticipates potential challenges, and envisions a successful outcome. They don't simply wander into the wilderness hoping to stumble upon success—they create a mental map of what success looks like and how they'll achieve it.

The same principle applies to entrepreneurial hunters. Before taking action in your business, you must see where you're going. Vision isn't just a corporate buzzword or a feel-good exercise—it's the foundation upon which all strategic action is built. Without a clear vision, you're not hunting; you're just wandering.

Visualization is more than positive thinking or daydreaming about success. It's a disciplined practice of mentally rehearsing your desired outcomes and the steps needed to achieve them. Elite athletes have used this technique for decades—mentally performing their routines perfectly thousands of times before executing them physically. As entrepreneurial hunters, we can apply the same powerful technique to our business pursuits.

When I started my lawn care business at eighteen, my vision wasn't just about mowing lawns. I visualized building a company that would provide exceptional service, grow through word-of-mouth referrals, and eventually expand beyond just me and my push mower. Each morning before heading out to my first yard, I would take a few minutes to see myself completing each job with excellence, interacting professionally with clients, and steadily building my reputation in the community.

This daily visualization practice wasn't simply motivational—it was strategic. It helped me clarify what success looked like in concrete, specific terms. It forced me to think through potential challenges before I encountered them. And perhaps most importantly, it programmed my subconscious mind to recognize and capitalize on opportunities aligned with my vision.

Effective visualization in business requires three key elements:

## Clarity

Your vision must be specific and detailed. Vague aspirations like "I want to build a successful business" or "I want to make a lot of money" aren't visions—they're wishes. A true vision includes details about what your business will look like, who it will serve, how it will operate, what problems it will solve, and what impact it will have.

Ask yourself: What exactly am I building? Who will it serve? How will it change the marketplace? What will my daily experience be like running this business? The more specific your answers, the more powerful your vision becomes.

## Emotional Connection

A vision that doesn't inspire you emotionally won't sustain you through the inevitable challenges of entrepreneurship. Your vision should create a genuine sense of excitement and purpose when you think about it. It should feel meaningful enough to justify your sacrifices to achieve it.

This emotional component isn't just about feeling good—it's about creating the internal motivation that will drive you forward when external motivation fades. When you deeply connect with your vision on an emotional level, you tap into reserves of energy and determination that others can't access.

## Actionable Pathways

While your vision should be ambitious, it must also connect to concrete actions you can take today. The most inspiring vision in the world is worthless if you can't translate it into specific next steps. Your visualization should include not just the destination but the journey—the key milestones, decision points, and actions that will move you from where you are to where you want to be.

This is where many entrepreneurs fail. They can articulate an exciting vision for their business but struggle to connect that big-picture thinking to daily actions. Effective visualization bridges this gap by mentally rehearsing both the outcome and the process.

The practice of visualization isn't just for beginners or struggling entrepreneurs. Even as my businesses have grown and succeeded, I've maintained a regular visualization practice. Before essential meetings, challenging decisions, or new initiatives, I visualize the outcome I want to create and the specific steps needed to achieve it.

This practice has proved valuable when facing unfamiliar challenges or entering new markets. By visualizing success in detail before taking action, I can identify potential obstacles, prepare for likely scenarios, and move more confidently and clearly during the execution of tasks.

Some practical ways to incorporate visualization into your entrepreneurial journey include:

## Morning Vision Sessions

Before diving into the day's activities, spend 10-15 minutes visualizing your most important objectives and how you'll achieve them. See yourself handling challenges effectively, communicating clearly, and progressing toward your larger goals.

## Strategic Visualization Retreats

Periodically step away from the day-to-day operations of your business for a more extended visualization session. During these retreats, revisit and refine your long-term vision, identify key milestones for the coming months or years, and mentally rehearse the critical actions needed to achieve them.

## Pre-Performance Visualization

Before essential events—sales presentations, investor meetings, difficult conversations, product launches—take a few minutes to visualize the successful outcome and your effective performance. See yourself communicating with clarity, responding well to questions or objections, and achieving your objectives for the interaction.

## Visualization Journaling

Write detailed descriptions of your business vision, including the outcomes you want to create and the process for achieving them. Review and refine these written visualizations regularly, updating them as you gain new insights, or circumstances change.

Remember, the goal of visualization isn't to escape reality but to prepare yourself to transform it. Effective visualization doesn't ignore challenges or obstacles—it anticipates them and mentally rehearses overcoming them. It doesn't replace action—it informs and enhances it.

As you develop your visualization practice, be honest about both your aspirations and the challenges you'll face in achieving them. See both the destination and the journey with clear eyes. This balanced approach to visualization will prepare you to hunt effectively in the complex and often unpredictable terrain of entrepreneurship.

In the next section, we'll translate your vision into a strategic business plan that will guide your hunting efforts and maximize your chances of success.

## Developing a Strategic Business Plan

An ancient Japanese proverb states, "Vision without action is a daydream. Action without vision is a nightmare." This wisdom captures a fundamental truth for entrepreneurial hunters. Once you've visualized where you want to go, the next critical step is developing a strategic plan to guide your journey from vision to reality.

This isn't about creating a rigid, 50-page document that gathers dust on your shelf—it's about mapping the territory you'll be hunting in and plotting your approach.

Many entrepreneurs resist formal planning, believing it stifles creativity or wastes time better spent on action. I understand this resistance—I felt it myself early in my entrepreneurial journey. Why spend time planning when I could be out making sales, delivering services, or developing products?

But I've learned that this view fundamentally misunderstands the purpose and power of strategic planning. A well-crafted strategic plan doesn't constrain you—it liberates you to focus your limited time, energy, and resources on activities that move you toward your goals rather than just keeping you busy.

Think of a strategic plan as a hunter's map and field guide combined. It helps you understand the terrain, identify the most promising hunting grounds, anticipate challenges, and develop effective tactics. Without this guidance, you risk wasting precious resources, pursuing the wrong opportunities, or using ineffective methods.

An effective strategic plan for entrepreneurial hunters includes several key elements:

## Market Analysis

Before you can hunt effectively, you need to understand the ecosystem you're operating in. This means developing a clear picture of your target market, including knowing:

- Who are your ideal customers?
- What values do your ideal customers have?
- What problems are in the market you are entering?
- What contributions will you make to that market?
- Who are your competitors?
- How are your competitors positioning themselves?
- What trends are shaping the market's evolution?
- What barriers to entry exist?
- How will you overcome those barriers?

This analysis isn't a one-time exercise—it's an ongoing gathering of intelligence about your hunting grounds. As a hunter constantly observes environmental changes, you should regularly update your market understanding.

Several years ago, I seriously considered entering the hemp business when it became legal in Kentucky. Instead of rushing in based on the hype, I took multiple meetings with people who had already invested in the industry and others who were also looking to invest. I examined the financials of companies for sale and those raising capital.

This research revealed something critical: there would be far more production than consumers could absorb. Additionally, neighboring states were moving faster toward recreational or medical marijuana. I recognized that people weren't going to smoke hemp if they could just cross the state line and purchase actual marijuana. I decided to give the market a year to develop before making any commitments.

That patience and thorough market analysis saved me from a significant loss. Many farmers who jumped in during the first big year haven't grown anything since. I avoided a tempting but unprofitable venture by understanding the complete ecosystem—not just the opportunity but the competitive landscape, regulatory environment, and actual consumer behavior—

When I expanded my lawn care business to include landscape design services, I applied the same diligence. I spent weeks researching the competitive landscape, talking to potential customers about their unmet needs, and identifying gaps in the market that I could fill. This investigation revealed that while there were plenty of lawn maintenance companies and high-end landscape architects in my area, there was a gap in the middle—affordable design services for middle-class homeowners who wanted something low maintenance but couldn't afford custom architectural plans.

This insight shaped my entire approach to the expansion, from my service offering, pricing strategy, and marketing messages. Without this market analysis, I might have tried to compete directly with established players rather than finding my unique position in the ecosystem.

## Differentiation Strategy

In a crowded marketplace, being good isn't good enough—you must be distinctive. Your strategic plan should clearly articulate how you'll differentiate yourself from competitors in ways that matter to your target customers.

This differentiation might be based on:

- Superior product features or quality
- More responsive customer service
- More convenient access or delivery
- More specialized expertise
- More personalized solutions
- More competitive pricing (though I generally recommend against competing primarily on price)

The key is identifying what your target customers truly value and developing a distinctive delivery approach. This isn't about being different for difference's sake—it's about being different in ways that create meaningful value.

## Resource Assessment

Every hunter must know their weapons, tools, and capabilities. Similarly, your strategic plan should include an honest assessment of the resources you can bring to bear in pursuing your vision, including:

- Financial resources (capital, cash flow, credit)
- Human resources (your skills, team members, advisors, contractors)
- Technological resources (systems, tools, intellectual property)
- Relationship resources (network, partnerships, channel access)

This assessment helps you identify leverage points (resources you can maximize) and constraints (resources you need to acquire or work around). It's about understanding what you must work with and how to deploy it effectively.

## Systematic Planning Process

As your business grows, having a structured planning system becomes increasingly important. Coming from a blue-collar background, I was familiar with "toolbox meetings" or production meetings, and I implemented these once I had employees. However, initially, these lacked structure and clear objectives.

Now, we use a hybrid version of the Entrepreneurial Operating System (EOS) across my various business interests. This framework has been invaluable in providing structure to our planning process. We hold strategic planning meetings quarterly, with one major annual offsite where we establish 2 to 3 strategic objectives for the year. These objectives then cascade down to 2-3 supporting objectives for each department.

This system provides clarity and alignment throughout the organization. Every team member understands what we're trying to achieve and how their specific role contributes to those objectives. It's created a rhythm of accountability through weekly "syncs" where we review scorecards and track progress.

I should note that you don't need this level of formality when you're just starting. But as you grow, operating with clear systems becomes increasingly powerful. The right amount of structure creates freedom by eliminating constant decision-making about the process so you can focus on outcomes.

## Adaptive Tactics

While your vision and strategic direction should remain relatively stable, your tactical approach must be flexible and adaptive. Your strategic plan should outline your initial tactical approach while acknowledging that these tactics will evolve as you gather feedback and encounter unexpected challenges or opportunities.

Think of tactics as the specific hunting techniques you'll employ based on conditions on the ground. Sometimes, you'll need to stalk quietly. Other times, you might set up an ambush, and on occasion you might need to pursue aggressively. The key is matching your tactical approach to the actual conditions you encounter rather than rigidly sticking to predetermined methods.

## Feedback Mechanisms

No strategic plan survives contact with reality unchanged. The most effective plans include explicit mechanisms for gathering feedback, measuring results, and making course corrections. Such plans might include:

- Regular review sessions to assess progress against milestones
- Customer feedback systems to gather insights from the market
- Financial metrics to evaluate business performance
- Team input sessions to identify operational challenges and opportunities
- Competitor monitoring to track changes in the competitive landscape

A strategic plan without these feedback mechanisms is like hunting with earplugs and blinders—you miss critical information that could help you succeed.

Developing a strategic business plan isn't a one-time event but an ongoing process. Your plan should be a living document that evolves as you gather new information, reach key milestones, or encounter unexpected challenges and opportunities.

As I've progressed in my entrepreneurial journey, managing multiple ventures from real estate to advertising technology, I've realized that intelligence at the highest level is simplicity. Who can say the most without saying the most? I'm currently in a phase of rolling back complexity in my businesses. The most sophisticated strategic plans aren't necessarily the most elaborate—they're the ones that distill complex realities into clear, actionable directives.

Remember, the purpose of planning isn't to predict the future with perfect accuracy—it's to prepare yourself to act effectively in an unpredictable environment. A good strategic plan doesn't eliminate uncertainty; it gives you a framework for navigating it successfully.

## Setting Goals That Propel You Forward

Vision provides direction. Strategic planning maps the territory. However, to move forward day by day, entrepreneurial hunters need something more immediate and actionable: clearly defined goals that translate grand aspirations into concrete action.

Goal setting is one of the most misunderstood and underutilized tools in the entrepreneur's arsenal. Many set vague, uninspiring goals like "increase sales" or "grow the business." Others set arbitrary targets disconnected from their strategic plan. Still, others avoid setting specific goals altogether, preferring to keep their options open or avoid the accountability that comes with clear targets.

But, the entrepreneurial hunter understands that practical goals are like the hunter's bow. This tool transforms potential energy into kinetic force, propelling you toward your target with precision and power.

Throughout my business career, I've found that the quality of my goals directly impacts the quality of my results. I make progress even through difficult circumstances when I set clear, challenging, strategically aligned goals. When my goals are vague, easy, or misaligned, I stay busy but rarely accomplish anything meaningful.

I experienced this contrast firsthand with different ventures. When I started Carroll Media, my advertising technology company, it began as a side hustle without clear goals. It took six months just to land my second customer, and growth was slower than it could have been because I wasn't setting specific targets. This experience taught me the importance of intentional goal setting, even for businesses that don't start as a primary focus.

## The Architecture of Effective Goals

Practical goals for entrepreneurial hunters aren't created equal. The difference between goals that propel you forward and those that leave you spinning your wheels lies in their architecture—the specific qualities that give them power and purpose.

The most powerful goals are simultaneously specific, measurable, challenging, and strategic. When I first expanded my lawn care business to include commercial properties, I didn't just aim to "get more commercial clients." I set a specific goal: "Sign contracts with five office parks with at least 2 acres each within 90 days." This specificity forced me to define exactly who I was targeting and what success was, shaping my prospecting, pitching, and follow-up activities.

Vague goals produce vague results. "Grow the business" isn't a goal—it's a direction. "Acquire 20 new clients in the commercial sector generating at least $100,000 in annual recurring revenue by Q3" is a goal. The specificity creates clarity, and the measurability creates accountability.

At the same time, your goals must stretch you without breaking you. I've found that goals with about a 60-70% probability of success tend to be most effective. They're challenging enough to demand your best effort but achievable and sufficient to maintain motivation. Goals that feel guaranteed success don't energize you, while goals that feel impossible tend to be demoralizing. This sweet spot is where growth happens.

Perhaps most importantly, your goals must align with your larger strategy. Each goal should represent a meaningful step toward your vision rather than a distraction. This alignment ensures that you're not just checking boxes but making progress on what matters most.

In my landscape design business, I initially considered setting a goal around building a large social media following. While this might have been interesting and even seemed business-related, I realized it wasn't well-aligned when I examined it against my strategic objectives—gaining more high-value residential design clients. I refocused instead on goals directly tied to generating qualified leads and increasing my design project close rate.

My approach to real estate investments followed a similar pattern of strategic alignment. Rather than setting arbitrary acquisition targets, I focused on gaining exposure to the real estate market through syndication—pooling resources with other investors to access better opportunities than I could, which aligned perfectly with my strategic objective of diversifying my wealth beyond my operating businesses.

Time-bound goals create urgency. Goals without deadlines are just wishes. Effective goals include a clear timeframe for achievement that prevents indefinite procrastination. These deadlines shouldn't be arbitrary but should reflect both the importance of the goal and the realistic time required to achieve it.

## From Goals to Daily Action

The gap between setting and achieving goals is bridged by systematic daily action. Many entrepreneurs falter here when they set impressive goals but fail to change their daily activities to align with these new targets.

To bridge this gap, I use a simple but powerful practice: identifying the 2-3 most important activities to drive progress toward each goal, then scheduling these as non-negotiable appointments in my calendar. These aren't vague intentions like "work on new client acquisition" but specific activities like "make 10 outreach calls to qualified prospects" or "complete and send proposals to the three pending leads from last week's networking event."

This practice ensures that your most important goals don't get crowded out by the urgent but less important demands that fill most entrepreneurs' days. It's about making time for what matters most rather than hoping to find time amidst the chaos.

What makes this approach particularly effective is the balance it creates across different dimensions of your business. Most successful entrepreneurs do not focus solely on financial metrics. While revenue, profit, and other financial goals are undoubtedly substantial, a balance with goals related to customer acquisition and retention, product improvement, operational effectiveness, team development, and personal growth should be present.

This balanced approach prevents the common trap of optimizing for short-term financial results at the expense of long-term business health and sustainability. It recognizes that a business is an interconnected system where progress in one area often depends on progress in others.

The final piece of effective goal execution is regular review and adjustment. I recommend a weekly review of short-term goals, a monthly review of medium-term goals, and a quarterly review of long-term goals. These reviews aren't just about checking progress but evaluating whether the goals remain appropriate as conditions change and new information emerges.

Sometimes, the most important outcome of these reviews isn't faster progress but the recognition that a particular goal needs to be modified or even abandoned in light of changing circumstances. The entrepreneurial hunter isn't rigidly committed to specific goals but rather to the larger vision and strategy they serve. This flexibility prevents the sunk-cost fallacy from keeping you committed to goals that no longer serve your bigger purpose.

Every goal needs an owner—a specific person responsible for its achievement. In a solo venture, that's you, but clear ownership becomes increasingly essential as your business grows. Without it, goals often fall into the gap between "someone should do this" and "someone actually doing it." Accountability mechanisms—regular check-ins, public commitments, external deadlines, or accountability partners—further increase the likelihood of achievement. I've found that goals I share publicly or commit to in the presence of respected peers have a much higher completion rate than those I keep to myself.

Remember, the purpose of goals isn't just achievement for its own sake—it's the transformation that occurs as you pursue worthwhile objectives. The entrepreneur who emerges from pursuing challenging goals is often more valuable than the specific outcomes achieved along the way. Each goal you set and pursue sharpens your skills, expands your capabilities, and transforms you into a more effective hunter. This internal transformation ultimately drives the external results that most entrepreneurs are seeking.

Setting goals with exemplary architecture, translating them into daily action, balancing them across key business areas, and reviewing them regularly creates the momentum that propels entrepreneurial success. It's not just about checking boxes or hitting targets—it's about making the trajectory that carries you toward your larger vision, one meaningful achievement at a time.

## The Value of Daily Small Wins

The path from vision to achievement isn't a single leap but through countless small steps taken consistently over time. While entrepreneurial hunters must keep their eyes on ambitious long-term objectives, their daily focus should be accumulating small wins that build momentum, confidence, and capabilities.

This approach contradicts the mythology surrounding entrepreneurship—the dramatic stories of overnight success, revolutionary breakthroughs, and heroic pivots that capture media attention and fire the imagination. But having built multiple businesses from the ground up, I can tell you that sustainable success rarely arrives in these dramatic moments. Instead, it emerges gradually through the compound effect of small victories consistently achieved day after day.

When I started my lawn care business with a push mower and a used truck, each new client represented a small win. Each positive review was a small win. Each referral was a small win. None of these individually transformed my business, but collectively, over time, they created the foundation for growth that eventually allowed me to build a thriving enterprise.

### The Compound Power of Small Victories

Small wins operate with surprising power on multiple levels. Most immediately, they create psychological momentum that fuels continued action. Success breeds success. Each small win triggers a positive psychological response—a release of dopamine that reinforces the behaviors that led to that success. This creates a virtuous cycle where achievement increases motivation, which drives further achievement.

Conversely, when entrepreneurs focus exclusively on distant, ambitious goals without acknowledging and celebrating smaller victories along the way, they often experience diminished motivation and increased frustration. Despite their efforts, the target seems to remain equally distant, leading to discouragement and sometimes abandonment of the goal altogether.

I discovered this principle when building Carroll Media, my advertising technology company. After the slow start, where it took six months to land my second client, I shifted my focus from obsessing about major client acquisitions to celebrating smaller milestones: successful pitch meetings, positive feedback on proposals, and incremental improvements to our service offerings. This shift in perspective created a sense of progress that kept me engaged during the challenging early phase, ultimately leading to the growth that previously seemed elusive.

Beyond the psychological benefits, small wins function as crucial skill-building repetitions. Each small win represents not just a step toward your goal but an opportunity for learning and improvement. Entrepreneurs who make five sales calls daily for a month don't just end up with new clients—they develop communication skills, objection-handling techniques, and market insights that make them more effective in future efforts.

This incremental skill development compounds over time in ways that often aren't visible but become decisive advantages as your business grows. The daily practice of key business activities—selling, problem-solving, communicating, and decision-making—gradually transforms you from an aspiring entrepreneur into a seasoned business hunter.

I've observed that the entrepreneurs who embrace this process of daily skill-building through small wins eventually outperform those with perhaps more natural talent but less consistent practice. It's the difference between the intermittent gym-goer with great genetics and the average person who never misses a workout—over time; consistent practice trumps sporadic brilliance.

## Strategic Risk Distribution and Feedback Acceleration

Beyond psychological momentum and skill development, the small wins approach offers two additional strategic advantages: distributed risk and accelerated feedback.

The small wins approach naturally distributes risk across many smaller bets rather than concentrating on a few large ones. If a particular initiative fails—as some inevitably will—its negative impact is limited, and the positive momentum from other small wins can carry you forward.

This doesn't mean avoiding larger initiatives when appropriate but approaching them as a series of smaller milestones rather than all-or-nothing propositions. By breaking down bigger objectives into small wins, you create multiple checkpoints where you can evaluate progress, adjust, and sometimes cut losses before they become catastrophic.

I applied this principle when diversifying into real estate. Rather than making one significant property acquisition that would have concentrated my risk, I participated in syndicated investments that allowed me to spread capital across multiple properties. Each successful deal represented a small win that built my knowledge and network while limiting my exposure to any project.

The small-wins approach also accelerates the feedback loop essential for entrepreneurial learning and adaptation. Small wins create frequent opportunities for feedback, allowing you to make course corrections before minor issues become major problems. Each completed task, each customer interaction, and each sales conversation provides data that can inform your next steps.

Entrepreneurs who pursue only big, infrequent wins often operate with limited feedback for extended periods, increasing the risk of moving in unproductive directions. By contrast, those focused on daily small wins constantly gather information that helps them refine their approach.

One of the most valuable questions I can ask after any business activity is: "What did I learn from this that can make me more effective tomorrow?" This simple practice turns setbacks into opportunities for improvement and accelerates the development of your skills and your business.

## Implementing the Small Wins Approach

Translating the philosophy of small wins into practical action requires the intentional design of your business activities. Here are the key implementation strategies I've found most effective across my various ventures:

First, break down larger goals into meaningful daily actions. Identify the 2-3 high-leverage daily activities for each significant goal that will drive progress. For a sales goal, this might be making a specific number of outreach calls or sending a target number of proposals. The product development goal might be completing a defined component or feature daily. The key is establishing a clear connection between daily actions and larger objectives.

Second, create visible tracking systems that make your progress tangible. Make your small wins visible through simple tracking systems—physical or digital. This might be as basic as a calendar marking completed activities or as sophisticated as a digital dashboard showing key metrics. The key is having visual confirmation of your consistent effort and gradual progress.

During the early days of my lawn care business, I kept a simple map of my service area and colored in streets where I had customers. This basic visual system allowed me to see my progress expanding across neighborhoods and identify areas with opportunity gaps. The gratification of coloring in new territory provided motivation that numbers alone couldn't deliver.

Third, establish daily minimums rather than maximums. Instead of setting a ceiling on your daily activities ("make no more than 10 sales calls"), establish floors ("make at least five sales calls"). This creates momentum that often carries you beyond the minimum while ensuring you maintain consistent forward progress even on difficult days. On many occasions, I've found that simply getting started with the minimum requirement often leads to exceeding it as engagement builds throughout the activity.

Fourth, deliberately celebrate meaningful milestones along the journey. At the same time, acknowledging all progress and celebrating milestones representing significant advancement. This might be signing your first client in a new market, reaching a revenue threshold, or completing a major project. These celebrations reinforce the connection between daily small wins and larger achievements.

Finally, institute a regular review process that extracts maximum learning from each small win or setback. Set aside time weekly to review your small wins, identify patterns in what's working and what isn't, and adjust your daily activities accordingly. This turns your daily actions from habitual routines into adaptive learning experiences that become increasingly effective over time.

The daily small-wins approach does require patience and faith in the process. In a business culture that celebrates overnight success and revolutionary disruption, the power of incremental progress can seem underwhelming. However, true entrepreneurial hunters understand that consistent, focused action over time creates results that appear miraculous to outside observers but are simply the predictable outcome of compound growth.

Remember, the most successful hunts aren't determined by a dramatic moment but by the countless small decisions and actions preceding the final strike. The hunter who masters the terrain tracks patiently, positions strategically, and acts decisively when the moment arrives is the one who returns with the trophy. Your business success will emerge from the accumulated impact of daily small wins compounded over time. This isn't just a strategy for achieving your goals—it's the fundamental rhythm of sustainable entrepreneurial growth.

# CHAPTER 3

# Growl and Grit: Building Resilience and Perseverance

*In the endurance of the hunter lies power, and in patience, victory. For it is written: the swift may begin the chase, but the steadfast shall claim the prize.*

*Behold, two hunters pursue their quarry. One relies on speed, the other on perseverance. When storm clouds gather, the first seeks shelter, cursing the skies. The second wraps himself in resolve and presses forward, each step a testament to his will. When traps return empty, and prey vanishes like morning mist, the first questions his worth. The second gathers the fragments of failure and forges them into wisdom that guides his subsequent pursuit.*

*As it is written in the testament of the wilderness: the swiftest river is halted by the fallen tree; the fiercest flame dies when it exhausts its fuel; but the hunter who masters endurance shall outlast all trials.*

*The prize falls not to the quickest starter but to the relentless finisher. The crown awaits not the talented who falter but the determined who persevere. The feast belongs not to those who merely hunger but to those whose hunger outlasts even the harshest famine. When the path rises steeply before you, will you retreat to comfort's embrace? When darkness stretches endless, will you wait for dawn or kindle your own light? When your strength ebbs, will you surrender or forge new power from the furnace of your struggle?*

*The glory of the hunt is revealed not in its beginning but in its completion. So it was, so it is, and so shall it ever be.*

# Growing Your Growl: Strengthening Your Resolve

In the wild, a hunter's growl communicates power, presence, and the will to dominate. In business, your growl is the unmistakable impact you make in your market—the unique force that makes competitors retreat and customers take notice.

## The Pursuit of Excellence

To be a great hunter, you must understand that mediocrity is not an option. The importance of not settling for less and not giving up—no matter how hard it may get—on your journey is essential to your success.

You should always desire more. Businesses are either growing or shrinking. They simply cannot tread water. This means that you must stay in a constant state of growth. But be cautious; if this is not your normal mindset, you will be judged. People will tell you to lighten up and calm down. Don't wear yourself out. This is all prejudice from people who don't understand their potential, nor have they ever tried to achieve it.

If businesses must always look to grow, so must the hunters who run them. You can push yourself to bigger goals and dreams if you believe you can achieve them.

That's not just some rah-rah self-talk bullshit, either. I honestly crippled myself in my 20s by not going bigger. I should have moved out of my small town sooner. I should have taken more risk. I should have pitched bigger deals. The downside to all of that is I lost that time. You can't take on the same risk at 33 as you can at 23. You have more to lose, maybe even a family depending on you. But that still can't stop you from wanting more. Never settle.

**REFLECTION POINT**: What area of your business or life are you currently accepting "good enough" when you could be pushing for excellence? What's one specific way you could raise your standards today?

## Closing the Potential Gap

Right now, you're somewhere between never even considering going out on your own and fully becoming who you were born to be. That space in the middle? I call that the potential gap—and your entire journey as an entrepreneur is about closing it.

Building a business isn't just about chasing leads or stacking cash. That's surface-level. The deeper mission—the one that truly separates the good from the great—is this: develop yourself.

Honestly? I consider sales more of a personal development skill than a professional one. Because to sell effectively, you have to understand yourself—your fears, your confidence, your ability to influence. Sales forces you to grow, not just show up.

And in the new era of business, change is constant. New tools. New platforms. New threats. The moment you stop evolving, the market passes you by. That's why learning can't stop. Self-discovery can't stop.

For the rest of your life, I want you to wake up every day and ask: How can I close the gap between who I am and who I'm capable of becoming?

That mindset will keep you growing. That discipline will create distance between you and your competition.

Because while others get comfortable... *you'll be sharpening your edge.*

# Building Your Brand in the Digital Age

What do you think of when you hear these names? Nike. Coca-Cola. Lays. Ford. More than likely, some slogan, commercial, or image came to mind. That means those companies have a brand. Growing your growl means building your brand. It's walking into a room and having a high percentage of people know precisely who you are. It's people seeing your logo and knowing exactly what you are about. The companies that can growl the loudest are the companies with the biggest brands.

The good news? It's never been easier or CHEAPER to build a brand. Right now, all you need to develop a personal brand is a camera and the audacity to hit the record button. Whether you're passionate about digital marketing, woodworking, fitness, or any specialized interest—there's an audience hungry for your expertise. With the influx of the internet, big brands are losing leverage every day. You now have a way to go direct to consumer.

Platforms like YouTube, Facebook, Twitter, Snapchat, and Instagram give the power back to the many. You no longer need to know someone in Hollywood to produce your own mini-series. Don't believe me? Spend an hour on YouTube. Plenty of people there are growing their growl!

# Finding Your Voice and Volume

So, here's the real question: how loud can you growl right now—and how loud are you *willing* to get?

In today's world, attention is currency. It's not about who you know—it's about who *knows you.* Donald J. Trump said it in *The Art of the Deal,* and it's even more true in the digital jungle we live in today.

Visibility isn't optional anymore. It's oxygen. And the louder you growl, the more oxygen you get.

At Carroll Media, we once ran ads for as little as $1.86 per thousand impressions. That's not just affordable—that's insane. For perspective, direct mail costs $400 to $500 for the same number of eyeballs. If that doesn't show you the power shift happening right now, I don't know what will. The game has changed. The loudest voice wins.

But let's be clear: this isn't about being obnoxious. It's about being *unignorable.* It's about stepping up, hitting record, and telling your story so clearly and consistently that people can't scroll past it.

So, ask yourself:

- Are you hiding behind perfectionism?
- Are you whispering in a world that rewards those who roar?

Don't wait to be discovered. Don't wait for permission. Find your voice, crank the volume, and show the world exactly who the hell you are.

Because the world doesn't need more silent killers. It needs hunters who *aren't afraid to be seen.*

## Leveraging Technology to Amplify Your Growl

The great thing about a brand—your "growl"—is that you can win people over forever if you build it right. The great thing about building a brand in the new era of business is being able to TRACK EVERYTHING. I can see how many people saw my brand and how many clicked on my ad to learn more from my site, and I can then target those people back on the web or social media sites for the next 180-300 days.

Having the ability to also target people based on their interests, income level, where they work, where they went to school, their level of education, marital status, and housing status, just to name a few, means that we are playing this business game at an entirely new level than ever before.

Listen, I'm a huge fan of cold calling—but you give me the ability to sell to people while I sleep, and I'm all in! We have taken it further and developed proprietary software at Carroll Media that allows us to go on the offense. Our bots (yes, like robots) are now engaging with our potential audience before they ever see an ad from us. It's all about growling the loudest in this new era of business. Coca-Cola has about a $3 billion marketing and advertising budget and has 2.4 million followers on Instagram. Tai Lopez, an entrepreneur who focuses on helping other entrepreneurs, has 2.9 million followers and has done that with far less than $3 billion.

## Collaboration and Cross-Pollination

Another huge benefit of the new era of business is the ability to remove geographic boundaries and connect with others. You can utilize this to help grow your growl by bringing in your comrades. Hop on a Skype call, Google Hangout, Facebook Live, Instagram Live, Periscope, or YouTube live and kick it with each other. Bring your fellow audiences some value, and you experience cross-pollination. Some of their audience will be new to you and your audience for them. If they like your content, they are likely to follow you.

This ideology in the social media world is that likes, follows, subscribers, and comments don't matter. I call bullshit. If you can command a person's attention to the level that they engage with you and your brand—you, my friend, have won. Remember, just like cold calling is a numbers game—so goes the social media game. Find industry experts with audiences similar to your clients and send them a DM to collaborate. This is the main reason I have my podcast—it's a way for me to reach out to influential individuals and offer to put them on a pedestal. There aren't many people that don't like to have their egos stroked.

> **REFLECTION POINT:** Who are three people in your industry whose audience overlaps with your ideal customers? What unique value could you offer them to create a win-win collaboration opportunity?

## Getting Comfortable On Camera

Have you ever recorded yourself on video? I'm not talking about home video style. I mean looking directly into that void of a lens and letting the person on the other end know exactly how you feel about something. Up until 2009, I hadn't either. And my first several videos were exactly what you should expect—terrible. What I have learned through the experience of being ok with being on video is this: You only get better by doing more.

Being on video is an excellent exercise for growing your growl. First, work on just using your phone to record a video; you don't have to get fancy with live video or anything like that. You don't even have to post your first videos if you don't want to. There are many schools of thought on structuring a video to post online. I personally don't care how you make the video as long as you do the damn thing.

Do you really want to knock your prospects off their feet? Take a quick 30-second video after your next pitch meeting. While walking out to your car, say something like this: "Hi Lisa—DJ here just wanted to say congratulations for taking the time to meet with me today to speak about the solution we can provide to solve your _____ challenge. I'll have that proposal over to you in the next 48 hours! Have a great day." Upload that to your YouTube channel and email them the link to the video. You will build your confidence while setting yourself light-years ahead of the competition.

## Visualization Techniques That Work

I have talked a lot about the power of thought in this book. That's because I truly believe that what your mind manifests into the universe, it will receive. You don't have to believe that, but like I always tell myself, what will it hurt? That's why I make visualization boards. A great way to grow your growl even louder than you think is currently possible is to create a board that can warp you into the future. I'm not talking about some Back to the Future time machine. I mean a board with everything you want—both in "things" and "feelings."

Having a board to look at will help you visualize your results. If you want a Porsche, put it on the board. Love the feeling of being on the edge where earth meets ocean? Put it on the board. Find all the things you wish were permanent in your life and visualize experiencing them daily. Cut out newspaper clippings, magazine pages, print photos from online, hell, glue a little sand to the poster board if you want. The idea is that this is YOUR vision board! Go wild with it, and then tweet me a picture of your board—@DJ_Carroll

In Jeffrey Gitomer's Little Red Book of Selling, he walks us through a process so simple and so elementary that it will have you scratching your head, thinking, "Is this guy crazy?" No. The only one crazy, in my opinion, is the one that doesn't take every actionable step this book turns you onto. I've literally read hundreds of books on sale in my research for writing this book, and one thing I didn't see much of was other authors giving due credit to other authors in their same genre. I'm not writing this book for me. I'm writing this book to help you get to the money fast, so if that means turning you on to "my competition," so be it. As long as you succeed—then I succeed.

Gitomer talks about writing the three biggest goals you want to accomplish on a 3x3 Post-it note. Then, there are three more secondary goals on another set of Post-it notes. I prefer to list six goals and then put them each on a different color note. To each their own. Gitomer then tells us to place these Post-its on our bathroom mirror so we are forced to look at them in the mornings and evenings. As you accomplish the goals, remove them from the bathroom and place them on your bedroom mirror. This will build momentum, and when you rise in the morning, you will see everything you have accomplished. This is a great exercise, and I didn't think this book would be complete without sharing it with you!

**Remember**: *Growing your growl isn't just about making noise—it's about making the kind of impact that changes the game in your favor. With each step you take to strengthen your brand, increase your visibility, and manifest your goals, your growl becomes more powerful. And in the business jungle, the loudest, most authentic growl always commands attention.*

## Learning from Failure and Licking Your Wounds

When you cut or burn yourself, it hurts. This teaches you not to take that risk or make that move again. The same happens in business. You're going to make moves and decisions that will hurt you. Some will hurt more than others, just as some lessons will have more impact.

Be mindful that you don't make the same mistake too many times. The faster you learn from a mistake, the quicker you can make the change so it doesn't happen again. Try to learn from others as often as you can. This takes letting go of your ego and admitting that you don't know everything, even when you have decades of experience. Don't worry about the emotional attachment of making the mistake—your emotions will try to keep you too safe. Live on the edge—get cut, bruised, and burned—but always learn from your mistakes.

## Understanding the Healing Process

Most of us know dogs lick their wounds, but do you know why? The enzymes in dog saliva help destroy the cell walls of dangerous bacteria. Studies show that antibacterial and antiviral compounds can be found in the saliva of both humans and dogs.

So why don't we lick our own wounds? Maybe because it's taboo in our society? It is ironic that being an entrepreneur has been taboo for many years, yet commerce and free trade are what economies are built on. Sometimes, you need to do things that are frowned upon to speed up your recovery from a wound.

In the entrepreneurial world, "licking your wounds" might look like two different approaches:

1. **When to push harder**: If you're dealing with a setback like getting hung up on during a call, the best remedy may be to hop back in and do it again

2. **When to take a break and recharge**: If you're failing because of exhaustion, you may need to step back from the hustle and grind.

Only you will know when to rest. You don't have to kill yourself—I find myself taking more vacations and more time off now than ever before. With that said, it's still not unusual for me to work 14-17 hours a day when I'm in grind mode. Being an entrepreneur is as much a journey of personal discovery as building a business.

# When Everything Falls Apart: My Elite Fitness Story

I've had my share of wounds to lick. One of the deepest came from what should have been one of my greatest successes.

I bought a fitness center called Wattsy's House of Iron from an owner who had lost his passion for running it. I purchased the equipment outright with a bank note and got the seller to owner-finance the real estate. We rebranded as Elite Fitness launched a supplement store with logo-branded apparel, coaching services, and dietary plans.

Everything was running smoothly. When I took over, the gym only had 100 members. Through strategic Facebook ads offering $1 trials that would auto-renew into $35 monthly subscriptions, I grew it to over 300 members in less than 18 months. The business was thriving.

Then came the day that changed everything.

A real estate agent— we'll call him Jerry— came in asking what it cost to build our building. He claimed he had a client looking for a similar property. As an entrepreneur, I quickly told him everything I had was for sale for the right price.

That was my mistake.

Fast forward six months, and we had a real estate contract signed. I had no representation or legal counsel. I simply took this guy at his word. We were supposed to have a confidentiality agreement, meaning neither would discuss the transaction until it was complete. But I later discovered that Jerry sat on the board of the buyer, which was a church.

Once the church announced, word spread through our small town faster than a California wildfire. Members started coming to the front desk asking if we were selling. My girlfriend at the time (now my wife), Victoria, who was running day-to-day operations, called me upset and panicked.

While under contract to sell the real estate, I was simultaneously looking to sell the membership and equipment to other local gyms. But once word about the real estate sale hit the street, I lost all leverage with potential buyers.

By January 2017, we had half the members we'd had in January 2016. I had to return the real estate to the original owner, who then sold it to Jerry and his client. I had to bathe on all my equipment, leaving me with about $18,000 worth of bank debt. I lost approximately half a million dollars in real estate.

I'm still proud that I never defaulted on that bank note. If you borrow money and give your word to pay it back, that's what you do.

By March 1, 2017, it was all gone—the business, the real estate—and I was left holding the bag.

I remember lying on the couch in the fetal position, whimpering and crying like a little bitch. That's when Victoria came over and told me this would be a chapter of our book. That failure was part of the process. I couldn't let this one-speed bump tear down all the work I'd put in for the past ten years.

I still had my real estate properties. I still had my power washing business. Nothing was left to do but lick my wounds and get back in the game. So that's exactly what I did—I grabbed my pressure washing rig from the shop and worked all night.

## The Lessons That Changed My Business Forever

From that experience, I learned several lessons I'll never forget:

1. **Always have legal representation**. There's no such thing as having too many attorneys.

2. **Make sure your paperwork is tight**. Jerry wiggled out of my lawsuit because the contract was vague and void of essential details.

3. **Your word is your bond**. Despite everything, I paid every dollar of that bank debt because I committed to do that.

4. **Having the right partner is everything**. Victoria showed me what every entrepreneur needs—someone who believes in you even when you don't believe in yourself, who picks you up in your darkest moments.

5. **Action heals faster than anything**. Getting back to work immediately was the best therapy I could have given myself.

This was a $500,000 lesson. Expensive? Absolutely. Worth it? In hindsight, yes—because I never made those mistakes again, and the lessons shaped me into a more innovative, more resilient entrepreneur.

## The Power of Your Why

Knowing your why is essential for multiple reasons, one being that it will keep you going during times of exhaustion. When I think I'm tired or when things are really hitting the fan, I think about my why. Your why can pull you through tough times.

Trust me—there will come a day when you want to give up. I don't care if you sell a product, perform a service, or just sell ideas. The day will come when you cut so deep that you just don't want to go forward anymore. This is when your why will matter the most.

You need to stop and think about how you felt when you started your journey. What made you want to step out on your own? What made you want to take the risk of being an entrepreneur? The answer can't be money. That won't sustain you through the tough times. The bigger your why, the more you will be able to endure.

My why is the Entrepreneur Institute. I want to build an Institute that trains entrepreneurs in every facet of business. That's going to take millions of dollars. Anytime I feel like giving up, I close my eyes and think of the thousands of people I could help with my why. That's enough to pull me through.

## Dealing with The Laughing Hyenas

As a hunter, you will face moments when your resolve is tested—not just by your doubts but by the sneers and laughter of those sitting on the sidelines, waiting for you to fail. These are what I call "The Laughing Hyenas." They're not predators themselves—they lack the courage—but they thrive on tearing down those who dare to hunt.

Albert Einstein said it best with his three phases of truth:

### Phase One: Denial

When you first set out on your journey, people will question your vision, ideas, and sanity. They'll say, "That'll never work," or "You're wasting your time." These are the naysayers who can't see past their limitations.

**Phase Two: Ridicule**

Once you've proven denial wrong by making progress, the ridicule begins. This is the hyenas' favorite phase. You'll hear things like, "It's just a fluke," or "They got lucky." The laughter can sting, especially from people you thought were in your corner.

Here's the secret: ridicule is a sign you're onto something. No one mocks mediocrity. The hyenas laugh because they're afraid that you're proving them wrong, afraid that you're succeeding where they've failed.

**Phase Three: Self-Evident Success**

Eventually, if you stay the course, your success will speak for itself. The same people who once laughed or doubted you will suddenly act as if they always believed in you.

The key to surviving the hyenas is to get through these three phases. You must build mental resilience. Expect laughter. Anticipate the doubt. Learn to see these reactions as milestones on your journey, not roadblocks.

# Understanding That You'll Never Be Perfect

I've said that perfection never arrives. Perfection is a word that doesn't belong in the business world. That's not condescending—it's setting your priorities sustainably.

Unless you're raising capital and selling your company every 36 months, you will need to be in this for the long haul. That means making mistakes but never giving up, always searching to reach your full potential, but never getting there.

When I bought Elite Fitness, I had never run any business in the fitness and health industry. That didn't hold me back from tripling membership, creating our own private-labeled supplement, and building a brand that dominated the local market. The fear of making a mistake could have crippled us, and none of that would have ever happened. What you create will tower over any mistakes along the way.

## Pain is Temporary, But Quitting is Forever

Every hunter faces pain. It's inevitable. Whether it's the sting of failure, the exhaustion of chasing a goal, or the heartbreak of a plan falling apart, pain will find you. But here's the truth: Pain is always temporary. It fades, it heals, it becomes a memory.

I've had moments when the pain felt unbearable. I've closed deals after weeks of rejection. I've rebuilt momentum after devastating losses. I've stood on stages when I wasn't sure I had the energy to get out of bed. Sometimes, the jungle of life and business felt like it was swallowing me whole. But every time, I reminded myself the pain won't last, but perseverance will. I pushed through and came out stronger, not because the pain wasn't real but because I refused to let it define me.

A hunter doesn't just survive pain—a hunter uses that pain. A hunter uses the pain to sharpen their instincts, deepen their resolve, and fuel their hunger. Pain becomes a tool, a teacher, and a stepping stone to something greater.

While pain is always temporary, quitting stays with you forever. When you quit, you're not just giving up on the goal—you're giving up on the person you're becoming. Every challenge, setback, and ounce of pain shapes you into the hunter you're meant to be. Quitting stops that process.

The next time you're in the thick of feeling pain, remember that the pain you're feeling right now is only temporary. It might last a day, a week, or even a season, but it will end. And when it does, you'll look back and be glad you kept going.

Quitting might feel like a relief, but it leaves a scar on your spirit—a reminder of the time you chose to stop when you could have kept going. Don't let that be your story.

Pain is inevitable, but quitting is a choice. Choose to push through. Choose to keep hunting. The jungle may be harsh, but it's also where greatness is born. And when you look back on your journey, the pain will seem small compared to the pride of knowing you never gave up.

## Making Failure Impossible

Failures are bound to happen. We are human; therefore, we will make errors in our judgments. These errors may cost you time, money, or both. But I don't think they are permanent. Failures are nothing more than lessons if you can find what you're supposed to learn from them.

People pay a lot of money for lessons. Don't believe me? Check the tuition rates at an Ivy League school. I can promise that there is only one way to fail. That is to give up. Instead, take your loss on the chin like a true hunter and study the lesson from the loss. Tear it apart and see what went wrong. What could you have done differently? Then, vow never to make that mistake again.

Too many entrepreneurs fail, not because of one singular mistake, but because they make the same mistake repeatedly until they are buried so deep that they have no other option to give up.

Remember: The hunter who learns from every track, every sign, and every pursuit eventually becomes the most feared predator in the jungle. Not because they never miss a shot but because they never miss the lesson.

# Harnessing Hunger: The Drive to Keep Going

By now, if you've made it this far into *The Hunter Head Game*, I'd like to think you're feeling a little hungry—not for food, but for the hunt, for the next big thing you're chasing down. Hunters, after all, are driven by hunger. This hunger is up with us in the morning and keeps us in the game.

But let's pause momentarily and ask: *Am I really hungry?*

Hunger is a powerful force, both biologically and mentally. In the physical sense, hunger is driven by a complex interplay of hormones and signals in the brain. When your body runs low on energy, it produces a hormone called ghrelin, which communicates with the hypothalamus, the brain's control center for appetite. This triggers a cascade of reactions that make you feel those gnawing hunger pangs, pushing you to go out and get what you need to survive.

As hunters, we can learn a lot from this biological process. Just as the body sends hunger signals to sustain life, your mind sends hunger signals when you're craving success. The question is, are you paying attention to those signals?

## The Power of True Hunger

From a scientific perspective, hunger is essential for survival—your body tells you you're running low on resources. But hunger isn't just about food. It's also about the drive to pursue what you need, whether closing a deal, hitting a personal milestone, or chasing a dream.

When you feel hunger in the metaphorical sense, it's a sign that you're wired for more. Your brain is lighting up with the same reward pathways that drive physical hunger, pushing you toward the pleasure of achieving your goals. The key is to harness that hunger, to let it fuel your actions and keep you focused on the hunt.

If you're wondering if you're truly hungry, here's a way to check:

1. **Do you feel a pull toward action?** True hunger compels movement. It doesn't let you sit still.
2. **Are you restless in your current situation?** Hunger thrives on dissatisfaction. If you're content, you're not hungry.
3. **Do you feel the urgency?** Hunger has a clock attached to it—an internal drive that says, *Let's go now.*

If you answered yes to these, then congratulations—you're hungry. And understanding and embracing this hunger is what sets hunters apart.

What happens when you stop being hungry? What's left when you lose that drive, that fire in your belly? The answer is stasis—a dangerous place where growth halts, ambition fades, and you start to settle.

As humans, we're wired to push forward, to strive for more. We can dream bigger, reach higher, and set goals that push us to become more than we were yesterday. When we lose that hunger, we stop fulfilling the very thing that makes us human—our ability to grow.

## The Danger of Settling

Settling isn't peace—it's stagnation. While finding balance and moments of calm in the chaos is vital, it cannot come at the cost of your hunger. True peace isn't about giving up the fight. It's about knowing you're in the arena, battling for something greater than yourself.

When you lose your hunger, you risk falling into stasis. Here's what that looks like:

- **Complacency**: Stop striving for more because what you have feels "good enough."
- **Lost Potential**: Without goals, you stop challenging yourself, and the potential for greatness fades into the background.
- **Regret**: The years pass, and you realize you left so much on the table—dreams unchased, opportunities missed, and impact unrealized.

Hunger isn't greed. Wanting more isn't selfish. Hunger is about creating a better version of yourself for the people and causes you care about. It's about being relentless—not just for personal gain but for your family, your community, and the world around you.

Imagine if great leaders, innovators, and changemakers had stopped being hungry once they'd achieved some level of success. What if Rev. Dr. Martin Luther King, Jr. had decided he'd done enough after one march? What if Elon Musk had stopped at PayPal? Hunger drives progress—not just for individuals, but for humanity.

## Finding the Ferocious Hunter

Regarding ferocious hunters, few are as relentless as Ken Griffin, the billionaire founder and CEO of Citadel. Griffin has built one of the most powerful financial empires in the world, thriving in the high-stakes environment of Wall Street. His ability to adapt and dominate, even during crises like the GameStop stock saga, showcases his razor-sharp focus and relentless drive.

Griffin's rise is a masterclass in ferocity. His success didn't come from sitting back or playing it safe. It came from staying hungry, anticipating his competitors' moves, and constantly pushing the boundaries of what's possible. Whether you admire his approach or not, there's no denying his impact and the lessons his journey offers.

But here's the real question: *Who is the ferocious hunter in YOUR world?* You don't need to be on Wall Street to spot ferocious hunters. They exist everywhere—leaders in your local business community, innovators in your industry, or even someone down the street running a small operation with big ambition. They're the people who don't stop—the ones who set the bar high and force everyone around them to up their game.

Recognizing ferocious hunters isn't just about admiration—it's about sharpening your game. You see what's possible when you study their moves, mindset, and drive. You get a front-row seat to what it means to be relentless, and that energy can inspire you to push harder in your hunt.

## The Benefits of Staying Hungry

I bet someone depends on you. That should drive you to stay hungry. As the hunter, you don't just hunt for yourself—you are hunting for the whole village or tribe. That sounds like a huge responsibility, but this will keep you moving. When I land a big sale for one of my companies, my family benefits, my team benefits, and my team's family benefits. Taking that ultimate level of responsibility will grow you as a person. Understanding that day in and day out, you need us ready to make decisions that could affect other people's lives.

*So, what would 10% more do for your life?* By now, you may be feeling a bit overwhelmed. Maybe you aren't sure if you want to continue in this fight or even get started. How do you eat an elephant? One bite at a time. All I need you to focus on is 10% more. Do 10% more in every area of your life over the next 3 months. If you are working out 5 hours a week, just do five and a half. If you are making 20 cold calls a day, just make 22. If you are checked in with your team or family 10 hours a week, just give me 11 hours.

Do this over the next 90 days and reevaluate what has changed, good and bad. I'd be willing to bet it's all going to be good. You are never going to be penalized by the universe for doing more. But doing more doesn't mean you must chart an entirely different course in life. Life is a big ship; it takes some time to turn around. 10% more per quarter puts you on course for a 40% increase year over year. Give it 12 months, and if it doesn't put you where you want to be, keep trying 90 days at a time. But whatever you do, don't settle. Settling is not an option.

## Hunger Creates Focus

In the jungle, a hunter without focus is just wandering. The same is true in life and business. Focus is the ability to tune out distractions, lock in on your target, and take deliberate action to achieve your goals. It's not just about working harder—it's about working with clarity and purpose.

Focus starts with knowing what you're aiming for. A scattered hunter wastes energy chasing too many things. However, the focused hunter chooses their target carefully, aligns their efforts, and takes the shot when the time is right. Without focus, even the best intentions fall flat. Distractions pull you in every direction, and your energy is spread so thin that nothing meaningful gets done. But with focus, every action has a purpose. Every step moves you closer to the goal.

Think of focus as your mental GPS. When you set a clear destination, it doesn't matter how many twists and turns come your way—you'll always find a path forward. But if your destination isn't clear, you'll spend more time wandering than progressing.

To create focus, you must:

1. **Define Your Target**: Be crystal clear about what you want. Whether it's closing a deal, launching a product, or mastering a skill, you can't focus on what you haven't identified.
2. **Eliminate Distractions**: Turn off notifications, say no to unnecessary meetings, and carve out uninterrupted time for your most important tasks.
3. **Prioritize Ruthlessly**: Not everything deserves your attention. Focus on the tasks and goals that have the most significant impact.
4. **Use the Power of Small Wins**: Break big goals into smaller steps. Achieving these creates momentum and keeps you locked in on the bigger picture.

Hunters don't get distracted by every rustle in the jungle. They stay locked in on their prey, waiting for the right moment to act. That's the mindset you need to bring to your work. Focus isn't just a skill—it's a discipline. And in a world full of distractions, it's your most significant advantage.

## The Power of the Sale

In the jungle, nothing happens until the hunter makes the kill. The kill is the defining moment—it sustains life, fuels the journey, and ensures survival. Business works the same way. No matter how much effort goes into planning, marketing, or strategizing, nothing truly begins until a sale is made. The sale is the kill, and it's the heartbeat of commerce.

Sales are the lifeblood of every business. Without them, there's no revenue, no growth, no momentum. A great product, a flawless strategy, or a fantastic team won't matter if sales aren't happening. The sale is where all the work comes together—where value is exchanged, and the real game begins.

Think about it: every part of a business relies on sales. Operations exist to deliver what's been sold. Marketing creates demand to drive sales. Even accounting is there to track the numbers generated by sales. Without a transaction, there's no reason for the rest of the machine to run.

Like a hunter must bring down prey to sustain the tribe, a salesperson must close the deal to sustain the business. The sale creates motion, keeps the lights on, and fuels the next hunt.

Commerce cannot exist without a transaction. No deal means no movement, no growth, no future. The hunt is only successful when the kill is made, and in business, the sale is the moment that turns potential into reality.

If you're a business owner, entrepreneur, or salesperson, you must ensure the kill. You're the one bringing in the deals, making the transactions, and driving the lifeblood of the business. Every call you make, meeting you attend, and pitch you deliver leads to this critical moment.

## Creating Hunger Through Challenges

Hunger is what keeps the hunter sharp, motivated, and relentless. It's the driving force behind every pursuit, the energy that pushes you forward even when the odds seem stacked against you. But hunger isn't something you always feel naturally—it's something you can create and cultivate.

You can build and sustain hunger in three powerful ways: not making a sale, working, and visualizing the sale. Each approach taps into a different part of your mindset, igniting the fire that fuels your hunt.

### Creating Hunger Through Missed Opportunities

Have you ever gone a day without eating? It's impossible to ignore that empty feeling in your stomach, the growling, the gnawing. The same thing happens to your professional hunger when you don't make a sale.

Not closing a deal isn't failure—it's fuel. It's a reminder that you're still in the jungle, that the work isn't done, and that the prey is still out there. The key is to channel that frustration, that emptiness, into action.

Think of this as fasting for your business. When you don't eat, your body craves nourishment. When you don't make a sale, your mind craves success. Instead of letting it demoralize you, use it to sharpen your instincts and redouble your efforts. The hunger you feel from not making a sale pushes you to chase the next one even harder.

## Creating Hunger Through Hard Work

Just as physical activity burns calories and makes you hungry, hard work in your business creates a hunger for success. When you're grinding, hustling, and putting in the hours, you're actively building the desire to see the fruits of your labor.

Think about the last time you worked on a big project or chased a significant goal. The more effort you poured into it, the more you wanted to see it succeed. That's the hunger effect. Every call you make, every meeting you schedule, and every pitch you deliver is like burning calories—you're creating space for hunger to grow.

Here's the trick: even if you're not seeing results immediately, working keeps you engaged and focused. It prevents complacency and keeps you in the game. Over time, this consistent effort builds momentum, and that momentum feeds your hunger to keep going.

## Creating Hunger Through Visualization

Have you ever walked into a kitchen and smelled a sizzling steak or freshly baked bread? That aroma immediately triggers your appetite, making you eager to dig in. The same principle applies to visualizing success in your business.

When you picture the sale—imagine the handshake, the signed contract, the satisfied customer—you're essentially "smelling the steak" before you eat it. Visualization is a powerful tool for creating hunger because it activates your mind's reward pathways, making the goal more tangible and achievable.

Close your eyes and think about the feeling of closing that deal. Picture the excitement of the client saying yes, the adrenaline rush when the sale goes through, and the satisfaction of knowing you delivered value. That mental image creates a pull—a craving—that drives you to take the actions necessary to make it a reality.

## The Company You Keep

As hunters, our success is determined by our hunger and the appetite of those we surround ourselves with. If you tolerate a lack of appetite in your circle, it will eventually dull your edge. That's why one of the most challenging but necessary decisions you'll ever make is auditing your relationships and cutting ties with those who lack hunger.

If you want to be a billionaire, you've got to hang around billionaires. If you want to be an apex hunter, you must spend time with other apex hunters. It's that simple. The people in your circle set the standard for what's normal, acceptable, and achievable. When surrounded by people with big appetites—those who are relentlessly pursuing their goals—it pulls you forward, challenging you to aim higher and work harder.

Conversely, tolerating people with no hunger—those who are content to settle or let opportunities pass them by—can drag you down. Their lack of ambition becomes contagious, sapping your energy and dulling your drive.

As you grow and evolve, it's essential to audit your circle regularly. Ask yourself:

- Who inspires me? Are there people in my life whose hunger motivates me to keep pushing forward?
- Who drains me? Are there individuals who lack appetite and bring negativity or complacency into my life?
- Who am I becoming because of my circle? Am I okay with that?

This isn't about being ruthless or cutting people off without reason. It's about protecting your energy and ensuring your environment supports your growth.

## Taking Bigger Bites

This lesson took me far too long to learn. For years, I was chasing numbers that were just too small. It took me three years to make my first six figures in business. And let me tell you, I'm not some know-it-all guru who got rich overnight. This has been almost 20 years in the making, and even now, I still get my ass handed to me from time to time.

But here's what I've realized: to be a beast, you've got to eat big. You've got to take big bites, make big moves, and dream beyond what feels comfortable. Beasts don't nibble—they devour.

For too long, I played it safe. I was setting goals that felt achievable, chasing numbers that were within reach. And while that worked for a while, it wasn't until I started thinking bigger— really *big*— that things began to change.

You see, small goals lead to small results. When you aim low, you're not challenging yourself to stretch, grow, or rise to the occasion. But when you set big, audacious goals, you force yourself to level up. You push your limits, and that's where the magic happens.

If you want to go to the next level, you must eat like beasts eat. And beasts? They don't hesitate. They don't overthink. They go after their prey with everything they've got. They take massive bites, and they don't stop until they're satisfied.

Big moves require considerable energy. They demand strategic planning, not just reactionary decisions. You've got to think beyond the immediate win and plan for the long game. This means asking yourself:

- *Am I chasing small wins or game-changing goals?*
- *Am I nibbling at opportunities or taking bold steps to devour them?*
- *Am I doing the work today that sets me up for a feast tomorrow?*

Taking big bites doesn't mean it'll always go smoothly. You're going to get knocked down. You'll make mistakes. But that's part of the process. It's part of growing into the beast you're meant to be.

I'm still learning this lesson myself. Even now, as I chase bigger goals and dream on a larger scale, I have moments of doubt and setbacks that sting. But I see progress every time I push myself to take that next big bite.

## Purpose As Fuel

When I was a senior in high school, I wanted to start my first business. I was excited, motivated, and ready to chase my dreams. But instead of support, I got resistance. My teachers and my guidance counselor didn't encourage my entrepreneurial goals. They pushed me in the opposite direction, encouraging me to give up my dream of starting a business and focus on becoming a chemical engineer instead.

Looking back, I understand their intentions—they wanted what they thought was best for me. But they didn't see the fire inside me, the hunger to create something on my own. That experience stuck with me, and it's why I'm so passionate today about giving back to young entrepreneurs, no matter their age—whether they're fifteen or fifty-five.

The path of entrepreneurship isn't easy. The learning curve is steep, and time is rarely on your side. When you're starting, especially as a young entrepreneur, you're up against the clock. Running out of money, support, or resources can quickly end your journey before it even gets off the ground.

This is why I deeply believe in helping those just starting. I want to be the person I needed back then—someone who believes in your dreams who supplies the information, tools, and encouragement to help you succeed. Because when you're early in the game, every bit of knowledge and support can make the difference between giving up and breaking through.

I've learned that your hunger is strongest when it's fueled by passion. Waking up daily with a purpose—something bigger than yourself—drives you to keep going, even when the odds feel stacked against you.

For me, that passion is giving back to entrepreneurs who are where I once was. The idea that I can help someone else avoid my mistakes, shorten their learning curve, or spark the belief that they *can* succeed drives my hunger.

Purpose fuels hunger in three powerful ways:

1. **It Gives You Energy**: When you're passionate about your work, the work doesn't feel like a grind. It becomes something you're excited to wake up and tackle every day.

2. **It Keeps You Focused:** A strong purpose keeps you locked in on your goals, even when distractions and challenges try to pull you off course.
3. **It Creates Resilience:** When your work is tied to something you care deeply about, setbacks don't feel like the end—they feel like a stepping stone to something greater.

## Making Burnout Impossible

Burnout is a reality for many, but I firmly believe that burning out becomes impossible if you have a big enough mission and purpose. Why? Because when your goals are massive—so ambitious that they'll take a lifetime to achieve—they naturally pull you through the tough times. The sheer size of your vision makes quitting unthinkable and ensures you'll always have a reason to keep going.

I've found that setting enormous goals can also act as an anchor against burnout. Big goals give you perspective. On the bad days—when deals fall through, projects fail, or you feel like you're spinning your wheels—those goals remind you why you're doing this in the first place. They pull you forward, past the frustration and fatigue, and keep you focused on the bigger picture.

To make burning out impossible, you need to:

- **Define Your Mission:** What's the big goal you're working toward? It should be so ambitious and inspiring that it lights a fire in you every day.
- **Stay Rooted in Your Purpose**: Remember why you started. When you reconnect with your deeper reasons, the work becomes rewarding, not exhausting.
- **Embrace the Journey**: Understand that big goals take time, and that's good. The longer the journey, the more

opportunities to grow, learn, and build something truly significant.

Hunters are defined by their drive, focus, and hunger for more. But just as important as understanding what hunters *are* is knowing what hunters are *not*. Recognizing traits that don't resemble a hunter is critical for staying on the right path—and avoiding behaviors that lead to stagnation and unhappiness.

**Hunters Are Not Passive**

Hunters don't sit back and wait for opportunities to come to them. They don't expect success to fall into their lap or rely on luck to guide their journey. A passive person avoids risk, fears failure, and prefers the comfort of doing nothing over the uncertainty of action.

But the truth is, passivity leads nowhere. A hunter knows that sitting still in the jungle doesn't just mean no progress—it means coming prey.

**Hunters Are Not Complacent**

Complacency is the enemy of growth. People who are content to settle for "good enough" rarely achieve greatness. Hunters are always looking for the next challenge, the next goal, the goal, and

On the other hand, those who lack ambition often find themselves dissatisfied with life. Without goals, there's no sense of purpose or direction. When you're not working, life feels flat and uninspiring from the pursuit, not just the destination.

**Hunters Are Not Reactive**

Reactive people wait for life to happen to them. They're driven by circumstances instead of taking charge. Hunters, by contrast, are proactive. They don't wait for problems to arise—

they anticipate them. They don't wait for someone else to make the first move—they create opportunities.

Being reactive is a sign of fear and hesitation, traits that have no place in the hunter's mindset.

**Hunters Are Not Distracted**

The jungle is full of distractions, and so is life. Hunters don't chase every rustle in the bushes or get sidetracked by shiny objects. They stay locked in on their goals focus on the task.

People who lack focus often struggle to progress because they're constantly pulled in a dozen directions. They say yes to everything and end up accomplishing nothing. Hunters know that focus is the key to efficiency and success.

## The Happiness Equation

I've learned that people are rarely happy when they're not chasing something. Goals give us purpose, and purpose gives us fulfillment. Without something to strive for, life becomes stagnant.

If you've ever felt stuck, frustrated, or unfulfilled, it's likely because you've lost sight of what you're chasing. Hunters don't let that happen. They set goals, pursue them relentlessly, and find joy in becoming better, stronger, and more capable.

The hunter's lesson is clear: the hungrier you are, the more you'll achieve. It's not just about wanting more—it's about having the drive, discipline, and determination to go after it. So, ask yourself: how hungry are you? And more importantly, what are you going to do about it?

# The Long Game: Playing for Sustainability

The streetlights had just flickered on, casting long shadows across the cracked concrete. It was just another evening in the neighborhood—muggy air hanging heavy, the distant thump of bass from passing cars, children being called inside for dinner. The house at the end of the block, the one with peeling yellow paint and a door that never quite closed right, always had people coming and going—a neighborhood fixture of sorts.

My cousin wasn't there to sell drugs that day. But in those circles, intentions don't matter much in that life. You're there, or you're not. You're in or you're out. And that day, he was in the wrong place at the wrong time.

They say they heard the boots on the front porch first. Heavy, determined footfalls that should have been a warning. Then the, splintering crack as the door burst, wood fragments spraying across the dim living room. Three men's faces concealed, weapons drawn. It wasn't about drugs, or territory, or respect—it was simpler than that. Money. They wanted money.

Words were exchanged. Threats made. Something escalated—a movement misinterpreted, a word taken wrong. And in an instant that stretched into eternity, a flash, a deafening crack, and my cousin was left bleeding and soulless.

Another young man - gone too soon.

I got the call around midnight. The kind of call that changes you forever, and splits your life into "before" and "after." I remember sinking to the floor, phone still pressed to my ear, my dad's voice breaking as he repeated, "He's gone, DJ. He's gone."

What haunts me most isn't just that he died. It's how easily it could have been me.

A few months earlier, my cousin had asked me to drop off a "video game" to a friend of his. I rode my moped across town, the case tucked securely in my backpack, never questioning why a video game delivery required such urgency or why his friend lived in a part of town my mother had always warned me to avoid.

It wasn't until years later that I realized what I'd been carrying. Pills. I'd unknowingly been a drug runner for my own cousin. I was lucky that day—lucky that no one stopped me, lucky that no deal went wrong, lucky that I wasn't in a situation where one misunderstood movement could end my life.

But luck isn't a strategy. And shortcuts in life are often the longest, most dangerous paths home.

## The Mirage of the Quick Win

In the streets, the drug game promises everything an ambitious young person could want; fast money, power, and respect. The dealers drive the nice cars, wear expensive clothes, and command attention when they walk into a room. To a kid with empty pockets and big dreams, it looks like success.

But what they don't advertise is the cost: the constant looking over your shoulder, the friends who turn into enemies, the prison sentences, and yes—the funerals. Too many funerals.

The same mirage exists in legitimate business. Get-rich-quick schemes. "Overnight success" stories. "Passive income" that requires no work. Shortcuts that promise everything without the grind.

The truth is harder but simpler: sustainable success requires playing the long game.

I've seen both paths up close. I've lost family to the short game. And I've built businesses—real, lasting businesses—by committing to the long game. The short game might get you a quick payout. The long game builds a legacy that can't be taken away with a single bad decision or stroke of bad luck.

## Understanding Time Horizons

Hunters understand that not every expedition results in a kill. Sometimes you track, wait, observe, and go home empty-handed. But these aren't failures; they're investments in future success. You learn the terrain. You study the prey's habits. You perfect your approach. And each hunting trip—successful or not—makes you better equipped for the next one.

The entrepreneur who plays the long game thinks in similar terms. They understand that:

1. **Compound growth always beats quick wins.** A business that grows 20% annually for ten years will ultimately dwarf a business that grows 200% once and then plateaus.

2. **Relationships outvalue transactions.** The vendor who consistently gives you a fair price for years creates more value than the one who offers a dirt-cheap price once and then disappears.

3. **Skills compound over time.** The knowledge and capabilities you build over years of dedicated practice create a competitive advantage that can't be bought or stolen.

4. **Reputation is currency.** Trust built over years of ethical dealings opens doors that no amount of money can unlock.

5. **Time reveals the truth.** Unsustainable business models, unethical practices, and hollow value propositions all collapse given enough time.

When I started my lawn care business at eighteen, my goal wasn't to make quick cash. It was to build something that would last—something I could grow, scale, and eventually leverage into other ventures. That long-term thinking is why I'm writing this book rather than hustling for the next quick score or, worse, becoming another tragic statistic.

## Mitigating Downside Risk

One of the critical differences between the short game and the long game is how risk is approached. In the short game, risk is often ignored or underestimated. In the long game, risk is carefully calculated and mitigated.

My cousin never saw the risk until it was staring him in the face in the form of three armed men. He was playing a game where the downside wasn't just loss of money or reputation—it was loss of life.

In business, the stakes are rarely high, but the principle remains: understand and mitigate your downside risk.

This doesn't mean avoiding risk altogether—entrepreneurship is inherently risky. But it means being clear-eyed about what you could lose and ensuring that no single failure can destroy everything you've built.

When I considered entering the hemp business a few years ago, I didn't just look at the potential upside. I analyzed the risk factors: overproduction in the market, regulatory uncertainties, and competition from neighboring states with more relaxed marijuana laws. After careful consideration, I decided the downside risk outweighed the potential gains and chose not to enter that market. That decision saved me from significant losses when many hemp farmers faced exactly the challenges I had anticipated.

The long game isn't about avoiding risks—it's about taking smart risks where the potential upside justifies the downside and where that downside won't destroy everything you've built if things go south.

## Unlimited Potential with the Right Time Horizon

When you play the long game, something magical happens: your potential becomes nearly unlimited. With enough time, consistent effort, and strategic persistence, goals that seemed impossible become inevitable.

Think about compound interest in financial terms. If you invest $10,000 at a 10% annual return, you'll have around $174,000 after 30 years—more than 17 times your initial investment. The power isn't in the initial sum or even the rate of return—it's in the time horizon.

Your business works the same way. Small, consistent improvements compound over time. A business that improves its operations, customer service, or product quality by just 1% every week will be approximately 70% better after a year. That's the power of playing the long game.

I've seen this in my entrepreneurial journey. Starting with a single lawn mower and a used truck, I built a business that grew year after year. That business created opportunities that led to other ventures, from real estate investments to marketing and technology companies. None of this happened overnight—each step built on the foundation laid before it.

## The Hunter's Patience

The most skilled hunters understand that patience isn't passive—it's strategic. They wait not because they're afraid to act but because they know precisely when to act.

As entrepreneurs playing the long game, we need this same disciplined patience. Sometimes, the best decision is to wait for market conditions to shift, your skills to develop, and the right opportunity to present itself.

This doesn't mean sitting idle. It means being productively patient—continuing to learn, build relationships, and improve your capabilities while waiting for the right moment to make your move.

When I was building Carroll Media, it took me six months just to land my second customer. In the short game, I might have given up, changed direction, or compromised on quality to chase faster growth. Instead, I stayed the course, focused on delivering exceptional value, and trusted that the right approach would yield results over time. Today, that patience has paid off many times over.

## Building a Legacy That Lasts

My cousin's legacy is a painful memory—a warning about the dangers of shortcuts and the brutal consequences of the short game. His choices, his environment, and, yes, some terrible luck combined to cut his story short. There's no business empire with his name, no children carrying his values forward, and no lasting impact beyond the grief of those who loved him.

That's the ultimate tragedy of the short game: it leaves nothing behind.

The long game is about building a legacy that outlasts you—a business that continues to create value, relationships that endure beyond transactions, and knowledge that gets passed down to others.

This doesn't mean sacrificing the present for some distant future. It means making decisions today that serve both your current needs and your long-term vision. It means building something that matters—something sustainable.

## The Entrepreneur's Choice

Every entrepreneur faces the same fundamental choice: play the short or long game.

The short game is alluring. It promises quick results, instant gratification, and the thrill of immediate success. It might even deliver on those promises—for a while. But it's ultimately unsustainable, built on shifting sand rather than a solid foundation.

The long game is more complex. It demands patience, persistence, and the willingness to delay gratification. Progress often feels slow. Results don't come overnight. But what the long game builds can withstand market fluctuations, economic downturns, and competitive pressures. It creates genuine, lasting value rather than the illusion of success.

I could have followed my cousin's path. There were moments when the quick money, the respect, and the apparent shortcut to success seemed tempting. But I chose differently. I decided the lawn mower over the drug deals, consistent growth over overnight riches, and sustainable value over transient gains.

That choice has made all the difference.

As you build your business, strengthen your brand, and chart your path as an entrepreneur, remember this: shortcuts are often the longest way home. Play the long game. Focus on sustainability. Build something that matters.

Because in the end, the true measure of success isn't how quickly you achieve it—it's how long it lasts.

## Your Long Game Strategy

To implement the long game in your own venture, follow these core principles:

1. Think in decades, not quarters. Make decisions that might not pay off immediately but create compounding value over time.

2. Build relationships, not just transactions. Invest in connections with customers, partners, and team members that strengthen over years.

3. Develop rare and valuable skills. Commit to the difficult work of becoming truly exceptional at something that can't be easily replicated or replaced.

4. Protect your reputation above all else. A tarnished reputation can undo years of work in an instant.

5. Create systems that scale. Build processes that can grow with your business rather than requiring constant reinvention.

6. Invest in your knowledge consistently. The most sustainable competitive advantage is your ability to learn and adapt faster than others.

7. Build with integrity from day one. Ethical corners cut today become structural weaknesses tomorrow.

The hunter's path—the true hunter—isn't about the quickest kill. It's about mastering the craft, understanding the terrain, and creating a sustainable approach that provides for your needs not just today but for seasons to come.

Choose the long game. Your future self will thank you for it.

# CHAPTER 4

# Kill Season: Mastering the Art of Business

*They track the same prey, these two hunters. One with perfect aim, the other with perfect words.*

*By nightfall, only one village feasts.*

*For the hunter who cannot convince lacks the final weapon. The meal belongs not to the skilled tracker but to the skilled closer. The tribe does not celebrate what could have been caught, only what was brought home.*

*In the sacred exchange of value, words become spears, conviction becomes currency. Doubt is the only predator that can defeat even the mightiest hunter.*

*To see is to begin. To approach is to continue. To claim—this is the hunter's true test.*

*The prey that feeds many is the one that was not merely desired but acquired. Vision without persuasion is merely a dream unfed.*

*When others hesitate, you must speak. When others retreat, you must advance. When others accept refusal, you must persist.*

*For, in the end, all hunters know this truth: Nothing exists until something is sold.*

*Outsell, or watch as others feast on your discoveries.*

*The choice is yours alone.*

# The Sales Mindset: Why Every Entrepreneur is a Salesperson

Picture this: A brilliant inventor creates a revolutionary product that could change an industry forever. The engineering is flawless, the design is elegant, and the potential impact is enormous. Yet five years later, this genius is still working out of a garage, barely able to pay the bills, while an inferior product dominates the market.

What went wrong?

The answer is simple yet profound: having the best idea, product, or service means absolutely nothing if you can't sell it.

I've seen this scenario play out countless times—talented entrepreneurs with groundbreaking ideas who fail not because their offering lacks value but because they refuse to embrace a fundamental truth: Every entrepreneur is a salesperson. Every. Single. One.

## The Ultimate Truth of Business

Let's get something straight right now—if you're in business, you're in sales. Period. It doesn't matter if you're a software developer, a restaurant owner, a consultant, or a manufacturer. It doesn't matter if you have a dedicated sales team or if you've never thought of yourself as a "salesperson." If you're an entrepreneur, selling isn't just part of your job—it's the cornerstone of your survival.

This isn't just theory. I've lived this reality through every business I've built, from Yard Smart Lawn Care to Carroll Media. My lawn care business didn't grow because I was the best at cutting grass—it grew because I could sell my services better than my competitors. Carroll Media didn't succeed because we had technology no one else had—it succeeded because we could sell our vision, approach, and solutions more effectively than others.

The marketplace doesn't reward the best solutions; it rewards the best-sold solutions.

## The Fear of Selling

I've met countless entrepreneurs who resist this reality. They say things like:

- "I'm not a salesperson—I'm a creator/innovator/visionary."
- "I'll build a great product, and it will sell itself."
- "I'll hire salespeople to handle that part of the business."
- "I hate selling—it feels manipulative and pushy."

This resistance often stems from misconceptions about what selling is. They picture the stereotypical used car salesman as pushy, manipulative, caring only about the commission. But that's not real selling. That's just bad selling.

True selling—the kind that builds sustainable businesses—isn't about tricks or pressure tactics. It's about:

1. Understanding a genuine need or desire
2. Offering a legitimate solution
3. Communicating that solution's value clearly and convincingly

That's it. When you strip away the negative associations, selling simply solves problems for profit. And what is entrepreneurship if not problem-solving for profit?

# What Happens When You Reject the Sales Mindset

Entrepreneurs who reject the sales mindset face predictable challenges:

- They build products or services that don't align with market needs
- They struggle to communicate their value proposition clearly
- They undercharge for their offerings because they're uncomfortable discussing money
- They lose to inferior competitors who are better at selling
- They blame external factors for their failures rather than addressing the real issue

I've seen brilliant innovators remain perpetually broke while mediocre entrepreneurs with superior sales skills build empires. Is that fair? Maybe not. But it's reality. And hunters deal in fact, not with how things "should" be.

## Embracing Your Role as Chief Sales Officer

Even if you eventually hire a sales team, as the entrepreneur, you are always the Chief Sales Officer of your business. You're not just selling to customers—to employees, investors, partners, suppliers, and even yourself.

Think about it:

- **Employees**: You're selling them on your vision and why they should commit their talents to your company
- **Investors**: You're selling them on the potential return on their investment

- **Partners**: You're selling them on the mutual benefits of collaboration
- **Suppliers**: You're selling them on why they should prioritize your business
- **Yourself**: On the tough days, you're selling yourself on why you should keep going

Every successful entrepreneur I know—from local small business owners to global titans—has this in common: they are exceptional salespeople, whether or not they use that label.

## The Hunter's Approach to Sales

Hunters don't agonize over whether they should hunt—hunting keeps them alive. Similarly, entrepreneurs can't afford to question whether they should sell. Instead, adopt the hunter's approach to sales:

1. **Track Relentlessly** - Identify your ideal customers and follow their patterns. Understand their pain points, desires, and behaviors.

2. **Position Strategically** - Place yourself where your customers are looking. Whether that's digital channels, industry events, or specific communities, be visible where your prey is searching.

3. **Move With Conviction** - When you engage, do so with absolute confidence in your offering's value. Hesitation kills more deals than objections ever will.

4. **Aim For Value, Not Just Capture** - The best hunters don't just take from their prey—they respect the exchange. Similarly, elite salespeople focus on creating genuine value, not just extracting money.

5. **Perfect Your Kill Shot** - Develop a closing approach that feels natural and effective. The moment of asking for the sale shouldn't be awkward—it should be the natural conclusion to a value-based conversation.

## Overcoming the "I'm Not a Salesperson" Mindset

If you're still resistant to seeing yourself as a salesperson, here's how to shift your thinking:

1. **Reframe Selling as Education** - You're not "selling"—you're educating people about a solution that can genuinely improve their lives or businesses.

2. **Focus on Problem-Solving** - Approach each sales conversation as a problem-solving exercise. Listen for pain points and demonstrate how your offering addresses them.

3. **Embrace Authenticity** - You don't need to adopt a "sales personality." The most effective selling happens when you're being authentic and genuinely helpful.

4. **Start Small** - Build your sales muscles with low-stakes conversations. Practice articulating your value proposition until it feels natural.

5. **Collect Wins** - Document positive outcomes from your sales efforts. Nothing builds confidence like seeing the tangible benefits your customers receive.

## The Ultimate Sales Truth

Here's the ultimate truth that separates successful entrepreneurs from the dreamers: Nothing happens until something gets sold.

You can have the greatest idea, innovative product, or revolutionary service—but until you sell it, it's just potential. And potential doesn't pay the bills, feed your family, or change the world.

The marketplace is the ultimate reality check. It doesn't care about your credentials, your intentions, or how hard you worked. It only cares about the value you deliver and your ability to communicate it persuasively.

Every business transaction begins with a sale. Every business grows through sales. Every business succeeds or fails based on its ability to sell effectively.

So, embrace it. Own it. Master it. Because the moment you accept that you are—first and foremost—a salesperson is the moment your entrepreneurial journey truly begins.

In the next section, we'll dive deeper into the hunter's approach to finding and closing deals, exploring practical strategies that work in today's competitive marketplace. But remember: a strategy without the right mindset is useless. The sales mindset isn't just about what you do—it's about who you become in the marketplace.

The question isn't whether you're a salesperson—it's whether you're an effective one. Because the hunting grounds of business belong to those who master this essential skill.

# Hunting for Clients: Finding and Closing Deals

In every hunt, there are two critical phases: first, you must locate your prey, and second, you must close in for the kill. Neither one is sufficient on its own. The most skilled tracker who can't close the deal goes hungry. The best closer who can't find prospects has nothing to close.

As entrepreneurs, our hunt focuses on finding and closing deals. This isn't just a sales technique—it's the lifeblood of your business. Let me walk you through the hunting grounds of modern business and share the strategies that have helped me build multiple successful ventures.

## Scouting the Territory: Where Your Clients Gather

The first rule of the hunt is knowing where to look. Wasting time in empty territory is a luxury no hunter can afford. Every market has watering holes—places where your ideal clients naturally gather. Your job is to identify these and position yourself strategically.

When I started Yard Smart Lawn Care, I didn't randomly knock on doors across town. I targeted affluent neighborhoods where homeowners valued their property appearance but lacked time to maintain it. I looked for houses with neglected lawns in otherwise well-maintained areas—signs of homeowners who cared but were overwhelmed.

Later, with Carroll Media, I hunted where businesses with digital advertising needs gathered—industry conferences, chambers of commerce, and online communities dedicated to business growth.

In today's marketplace, client watering holes exist in both physical and digital spaces:

**Physical Hunting Grounds:**

- Industry conferences and trade shows
- Professional networking events
- Chambers of Commerce meetings
- Exclusive clubs and associations

- Complementary businesses (partnerships and referral sources)

## Digital Hunting Grounds:

- Industry-specific online forums and communities
- LinkedIn and other professional social networks
- Facebook groups centered around your target market's interests
- YouTube comment sections of relevant content
- Reddit subreddits focused on your industry or solution

The key is to hunt where the prey is plentiful, and the competition is either absent or ineffective. Too many entrepreneurs waste valuable time and resources in depleted territories while rich hunting grounds remain untapped.

## The Long Game: Persistence in the Hunt

Some prey is worth tracking for years. My first significant client acquisition was BRG Apartments out of Cincinnati. To this day, I still consider Jeff March one of my very first foundational mentors. I tried to land one of their apartment communities, and it took me three years to finally break through—three years worth of calling on them, showing up, and staying in front of them—before they finally allowed me to place a bid.

But when I landed the bid, it wasn't just for one property. It was for five. It was a huge game changer and pays tribute to the fact that you must keep hunting, showing up, and demonstrating value. The biggest deals often go to the hunter with the most patience and persistence.

Too many entrepreneurs give up after a few rejections, not realizing that the big game often requires sustained pursuit over time. If I had quit after the first year—or even the second—I would have missed the contract that transformed my business.

## Tracking Signals: Identifying Ready-to-Buy Prospects

A skilled hunter doesn't chase every animal in the forest. They look for specific signals—tracks, markings, behaviors—that indicate which prey is worth pursuing.

In business, specific signals indicate prospects who are more likely to buy. Learning to spot these can dramatically increase your success rate while reducing wasted effort:

**Pain Signals:**

- Complaints about current providers or solutions
- Public expressions of frustration with specific problems
- Questions in forums or social media seeking solutions
- Emergencies requiring immediate assistance

**Opportunity Signals:**

- New funding or budget approvals
- Growth announcements or expansion plans
- New leadership or strategic initiatives
- Regulatory changes affecting their business

**Readiness Signals:**

- Detailed questions about implementation or specifics
- Requests for case studies or references
- Mentions of timeframes or deadlines

- Direct inquiries about pricing or contracts

The most successful hunters aren't those who pursue the most prey—they're those who seek the right prey at the right time.

## The Art of the Approach: Making First Contact

Once you've spotted your prey, the approach is critical. Move too aggressively, and your prey will flee. Approach too timidly, and your prey won't take you seriously.

Your first contact with a prospect in business often determines the entire relationship trajectory. Here's how to approach like a master hunter:

**1. Research Before Contact:** Before reaching out to any prospect, I understand their business, challenges, and potential needs. When I approach business owners for Carroll Media, I review their existing digital presence, identify specific improvement opportunities, and reference these in my initial outreach. This preparation demonstrates respect for their time and immediately differentiates you from the salespeople who lead with generic pitches.

**2. Lead with Value, Not Requests**: The amateur salesperson asks for something immediately: "Can I have 15 minutes of your time?" The hunter offers something of value first: "I noticed your Google ads are displaying incorrectly on mobile devices—here's a quick fix that might help."

When I first contact a prospect, I always provide something useful: insight, information, or a small solution to an existing problem. This establishes you as a valuable resource, not just another vendor seeking their money.

**3. The Power of Personalization**: The digital age has transformed how we research prospects. Today, you can know more about someone before your first conversation than salespeople of previous generations knew after multiple meetings.

I've found that LinkedIn is a goldmine for this—not just for professional information but for personal insights. You can discover a prospect's favorite books, causes they care about, and standard connections that can serve as conversation starters or reference points. This isn't about manipulation; it's about finding genuine connection points.

As I always say, an ounce of preparation is worth a pound of execution. Ten minutes spent researching a prospect can save wasted hours in misdirected pitches.

## The SOSC Method: A Framework for Closing

Over the years, I've developed a closing framework that has proven effective across industries and client types. I call it: The SOSC Method:

**S – Struggle:** Identify the client's genuine struggle. Clients typically don't buy unless they solve a problem or address a pain point. Right out of the gate, I want to focus on their challenges, not my product. I ask questions and listen intently to understand what's keeping them up at night.

**O – Opportunity:** Once I understand their struggle, I work with them to identify the opportunity and what could be possible if we addressed it effectively. This creates a vision of a better future that becomes the motivation for change.

**S – Solution:** Only after fully understanding their struggle and the opportunity do I present my solution—whether that's an estimate, quote, or proposal. The solution is directly tied to what we've already discussed, making it feel custom-tailored to their specific needs.

**C – Close:** Finally, I ask for the business directly and clearly. You must ask for the business, and don't be afraid to press a little at the right time. I like to say, "The makers make, the takers take." Big ballers know how to ask for business and are not afraid to press a little at the right time in the conversation.

This framework ensures that I'm solving real problems, not just pitching products and that the close feels like the natural next step rather than a high-pressure tactic.

## The Kill Zone: Closing Techniques That Work

Finding prospects and making contact are just the preliminaries. The defining moment of the hunt is the close—that critical point where interest transforms into commitment.

Many entrepreneurs feel uncomfortable at this stage. They track effectively and approach skillfully but then hesitate at the crucial moment. Here are the closing techniques that have proven most effective in my business journey:

**1. The Assumptive Close:** Rather than asking if they want to buy, assume they do and focus on the implementation details: "Based on what we've discussed, it seems the comprehensive package would best address your needs. Should we schedule your first service for next Tuesday, or would Thursday work better?" This subtle shift bypasses the yes/no decision and moves the conversation to logistics. I've used this successfully throughout my career, from lawn care to marketing services.

**2. The Summary Close:** Summarize everything the prospect has told you about their problems and how your solution addresses each point: "You mentioned struggling with inconsistent quality from your current provider, concerns about response time, and the need for better reporting. Our service addresses each of these by... Does that sound like the solution you're looking for?" This technique is powerful because it uses the prospect's own words to demonstrate the value of your offering.

**3. The Alternative Choice Close:** Instead of asking for a yes or no, offer two positive options: "Would you prefer the monthly maintenance plan or the quarterly deep service?" This approach acknowledges that the client is choosing your service and simply deciding on the details.

**4. The Urgency Close:** Create legitimate reasons why acting now is beneficial: "We're scheduled to implement a price increase next month" or "Our schedule for new clients is filling up quickly for the spring season." The key word here is legitimate. False urgency damages trust.

**5. The Trial Close:** Test the prospect's readiness throughout the conversation: "How does this sound so far?" or "Is this addressing your main concern?" These check-in questions help you gauge interest and address objections before the final close.

I often use multiple closing techniques in the same conversation in my businesses, adjusting based on the prospect's responses and the specific situation.

## Embracing Rejection as Part of the Process

Rejection is just part of the process. I can't tell you how many times I've been told no. There's a great book called "Go for No" by Richard Fenton and Andrea Waltz (I had them as guests on The Sales Factory podcast—you can check that out at CoachCarroll.com/podcast).

I always say your job as a salesperson doesn't start until you hear the word "no." That's when the real work begins. Too many entrepreneurs take rejection personally or see it as a final answer rather than the beginning of a conversation.

The hunters who feast most often pursue multiple prey, expect rejection as part of the process, and keep moving forward regardless. They understand that "no" often means "not now" or "I need more information" rather than "never."

## After the Kill: Turning One Deal into Many

The greatest hunters don't exhaust themselves with a constant pursuit of new prey. They maximize the value of each successful hunt.

In business terms, this means:

**1. Immediate Upsells and Cross-Sells**: Clients who have decided to buy are more receptive to additional offers. When I signed new lawn care clients, I would immediately offer complementary services like fertilization programs or seasonal clean-ups.

**2. Systematic Referral Requests**: I will shout out to Hayk Tadevosyan, a successful insurance agent who told me that if a team member doesn't ask for referrals at the end of a call, they owe him 100 cold calls. That's savage but brilliant. After owing that penalty a few times, you never forget to ask for referrals again. Referrals are pretty simple. You just have to be strategic about it and consistent. One of my favorite tracks to use is: "Mr./Mrs. Client, do you know anyone else who could use our [insert your product/service]?" It is straightforward but effective when used consistently.

**3. Testimonial Capture:** Create a system for collecting and showcasing client success stories. These become powerful weapons for future hunts. After completing projects for Carroll Media clients, we have a specific process for documenting results and requesting testimonials.

**4. Strategic Check-Ins:** Schedule regular value-add touchpoints that aren't sales-focused. These maintain the relationship and create natural opportunities for additional business. My team schedules quarterly review calls with clients to provide insights and identify new opportunities.

## The Hunter's Closing Mindset

Beyond specific techniques, successful closing requires the right mindset. Here's what I've observed in the most effective closers:

**1. Conviction Overcomes Objection:** If you don't fully believe in your offering, prospects will sense your doubt. The most powerful closing tool is absolute conviction in the value you provide. When I sell, I remember the clients whose businesses or lives have been transformed by what I offer. That genuine belief comes through in every word and gesture.

**2. Silence Is a Weapon:** After asking for the sale, shut up. Many deals are lost because the salesperson gets nervous and keeps talking, giving the prospect reasons to hesitate. I've closed major deals simply by asking the question and then waiting patiently for the answer, no matter how uncomfortable the silence becomes.

**3. Rejection Is Information, Not Failure:** Every "no" teaches you something valuable—about your offering, communication, or prospect selection. The best hunters don't take rejection personally; they use it as intelligence for the next hunt.

**4. The Close Begins at the Opening:** Closing isn't a technique you deploy at the end of a conversation—it's a process that begins with your first interaction. Every question you ask, every benefit you highlight, and every objection you address is part of creating the path to a natural, logical close.

## Find Your Hunting Style

There is no one-size-fits-all approach to hunting clients. The most successful entrepreneurs develop a style that aligns with their strengths and market.

My approach has always been high-touch and relationship-focused, even as we've incorporated digital tools. I build trust through demonstrated expertise and genuine interest in my clients' success. Other successful hunters I know take different approaches—some are more analytical and data-driven, others more charismatic and inspirational.

The key is authenticity. Your hunting style must feel natural and align with who you are. Prospects can sense incongruence; nothing kills a deal faster than appearing inauthentic.

Find your authentic hunting style, then refine and strengthen it with deliberate practice. The most successful client hunters aren't those with the most natural talent—they consistently study their craft, learn from each hunt, and relentlessly improve their approach.

In the next section, we'll explore how to adapt your hunting techniques as market conditions change—because the terrain constantly shifts, and the hunters who thrive are those who evolve along with it.

## Adapting to Market Trends and Consumer Behavior

In the wilderness of commerce, only the most adaptable survive. The hunter who sees the shifting winds, who reads the changing terrain, who understands the movement of prey before the movement begins, is the hunter who feasts.

Markets are living, breathing ecosystems. They shift like shadows, morph like water, and change with speed, which can devour the unprepared. The entrepreneur who fails to adapt is no different from the hunter who ignores the changing patterns of migration—doomed to starve, irrelevant, forgotten.

## The Predator's Perspective on Market Intelligence

When I started Yard Smart, I believed having a great service was excellent enough. I could cut grass better than anyone. I could design landscapes that would make homeowners weep with joy. But greatness isn't about being the best but being the most aware.

Market intelligence isn't a luxury. It's survival.

Consider the hemp business I almost entered. While other entrepreneurs were rushing in, blindly believing the green rush would last forever, I took a different approach. I didn't just look at the surface-level excitement. I dove deep:

- I met with multiple investors already in the industry
- I examined the financials of companies for sale
- I analyzed the production landscape
- I looked at regulatory environments in neighboring states

What I discovered wasn't what others saw. While everyone focused on production, I saw a critical problem: there would be far more production than consumers could possibly absorb. Neighboring states were moving faster on recreational marijuana, which meant people wouldn't settle for hemp when they could get the real thing just across state lines.

The result? I avoided a potentially catastrophic investment while others rushed in blindly.

## Reading the Consumer's Mind

Understanding consumer behavior isn't mystical—it's strategic. It's about seeing beyond what people say and understanding what they truly want.

Take social media as an example. Most businesses see it as a marketing channel. The hunter sees it as a real-time focus group, a direct line into the consumer's psyche. Platforms like Instagram, YouTube, and TikTok aren't just places to post content—they're landscapes of consumer desire, frustration, and evolution.

### The Three Layers of Consumer Insight

1. **Surface Level:** What consumers say they want
2. **Emotional Level:** What consumers feel
3. **Unconscious Level:** What consumers don't even know they need yet

The most successful entrepreneurs operate at the third level. They don't just respond to market trends—they anticipate them.

## The Danger of Rigidity

The business landscape is littered with cautionary tales of companies that refused to adapt. Entire industries have been disrupted overnight by those willing to challenge the status quo and embrace change. The moment you believe you have everything figured out is the moment you begin your descent.

Rigidity is the hunter's greatest enemy. In the jungle of business, those who cannot bend will inevitably break. Successful entrepreneurs understand that adaptability isn't just a strategy—it's a survival mechanism.

## Adaptive Strategies for the Modern Hunter

### 1. Continuous Learning

- Read voraciously across industries
- Attend conferences outside your primary field
- Listen to podcasts from diverse perspectives
- Engage with people who think differently

### 2. Flexible Execution

- Create systems that can pivot quickly
- Maintain cash reserves for unexpected opportunities
- Build a team that values adaptability over experience

### 3. Predictive Intelligence

- Use data, not just intuition
- Develop multiple scenario plans
- Create key performance indicators (KPIs) that signal market shifts early

### 4. Embrace Technological Evolution

The internet has demolished geographic boundaries. A business in Louisville can now compete globally with minimal overhead. But this requires constant technological adaptation.

At Carroll Media, we've developed proprietary software called Alli. She gets installed on your website and can then identify anonymous visitors by name, email, phone number, and sometimes even physical address. The game has changed, and we are helping change it for businesses across the US.

## The Hunter's Adaptation Manifesto

- Markets will change. Always.
- Your first strategy will never be your final strategy.
- Comfort is the enemy of growth.
- Learn faster than your competition.
- See change as an opportunity or threat.

# The AI Revolution: Adapting to the Most Disruptive Technology

My buddy Tyler Jenkins recently asked me how I keep up with all the changes in artificial intelligence. My answer was simple: voracious learning. You must make time to learn, to analyze and most importantly, to use these new platforms.

Artificial Intelligence isn't just another technological trend. It's a fundamental reshaping of how we do business, how we think, and solve problems. But here's the critical insight: AI is a tool, not a replacement. The hunter who masters AI isn't the one who fears it, but the one who learns to wield it like the most precise weapon in their arsenal.

## The AI Adaptation Playbook

1. **Curiosity is Your Competitive Advantage:** I spend hours playing with AI tools, asking questions, testing boundaries. Not because I'm a tech wizard, but because I'm endlessly curious. The moment you stop learning is the moment you become obsolete.

2. **Humble Intelligence:** The smartest move? Surround yourself with people smarter than you. When it comes to AI, I'm constantly reaching out to experts, asking questions, and absorbing insights. Pride has no place in learning—especially with technology evolving so rapidly.

3. **Practical Application, Not Hype:** AI isn't about fancy demos or theoretical potential. It's solving real problems. In Carroll Media, we're not just talking about AI—we're using it to:
   - Generate initial content drafts
   - Analyze market trends
   - Create more targeted marketing strategies
   - Streamline communication processes

4. **Ethical Adaptation:** The most powerful hunters understand that technology is a responsibility, not just a tool. The true master doesn't just use the technology—they consider its broader implications.

## The AI Revolution is Here

Artificial Intelligence is the most significant business transformation since the internet and there after social media. But it's not about replacing human intelligence—it's about *augmenting* it.

Think of AI like a highly skilled hunting partner. It can track data across impossible distances, spot patterns you'd never see, and provide insights that would take humans months or years to uncover. However, a hunter still needs to make the final decision, interpret the insights, and determine the strategy.

The Warning: Those who ignore AI will be left behind. Those who blindly follow AI without critical thinking will be misled. The winners? Those who learn to dance with the technology—guiding, challenging, and using it to see around corners.

## Preparing for the Next Hunt

Adaptation is only the first step. Once you've learned to read the terrain, understand the shifts, and position yourself strategically, you'll inevitably face your next challenge: the objections that may stand between you and your kill.

The true test of a hunter isn't just in seeing the opportunity. It's overcoming the obstacles that keep you from seizing it. Every objection is a wall. Every doubt is a barrier. And in the next phase of our hunt, we'll learn how to tear down those walls, silence those doubts, and close the distance between possibility and victory.

The market has changed. The prey has evolved. And now, it's time to learn how to overcome every obstacle between you and success.

Are you ready to turn objections into opportunities?

## Overcoming Common Sales Objections

Every hunter faces resistance. It's inevitable. When you close in for the kill, something changes—your prey senses danger and prepares to flee. In the jungle of business, this resistance takes the form of objections. The prospect who was nodding along suddenly throws up barriers, hesitates, and pulls back from the sale.

This is the moment that separates true hunters from the hunted.

This is the crucible where entrepreneurs are forged.

## Rejection: The Gateway to Success

Let me tell you something that might initially sound strange: You're not truly in business until you've been rejected. You're not really in sales until you've heard the word "no" more times than you can count.

That statement might seem harsh, but it's one of this book's most essential truths. The ability to face rejection—to hear "no" and keep moving forward—separates the dreamers from the doers, the wannabes from the real entrepreneurs.

I've seen countless talented people with brilliant ideas who never built the business they could. Not because they lacked skills or intelligence but because they couldn't handle hearing "no." The first sign of resistance sent them back to the safety of the known, back to the comfort of their 9-to-5, back to a life where rejection could have been avoided.

But they never understood that rejection isn't the end of the journey—it's the beginning. It's the initiation ritual that every successful entrepreneur must pass through. The more comfortable you get with hearing "no," the closer you get to success.

As my mentor used to tell me, "Your job as a salesperson doesn't truly begin until you hear the word 'no.'" That's when the real work starts. That's when you prove your worth as a hunter.

## The Twin Fears That Keep People Small

In my years of coaching entrepreneurs, I've identified two primary fears that keep people from pursuing their dreams:

1. **The Fear of Success** - Believe it or not, many people are terrified of achieving their goals. They worry about the new expectations that will come with success. "If I reach the top of the mountain, everyone will expect me to stay there." The pressure of maintaining success feels overwhelming, so they never even start the climb.

2. **The Fear of Rejection** - This is the big one. The fear of hearing "no," of facing criticism, of being ridiculed or dismissed. It's not just about professional rejection but the social and emotional impact of putting yourself out there and having people push back.

These twin fears keep potentially great entrepreneurs stuck in mediocre lives. They keep hunters from ever leaving the safety of the village to pursue their prey.

But here's the truth: Both fears are illusions. Success isn't a cliff you fall off—it's a journey that continues to evolve. And rejection isn't fatal—it's just information that helps you refine your approach.

## Why Objections Are a Gift

When a prospect objects, your first reaction might be disappointment. You might see it as a roadblock, a sign that the deal is slipping away. But top performers—true hunters—see objections differently.

An objection isn't a "no"—it's a request for more information. It's a signal that the prospect is engaged enough to raise concerns. It's an opportunity to address specific issues holding them back from saying "yes."

Think about it this way: The prospect who raises objections is giving you a roadmap to closing the deal. They're telling you exactly what's standing in your way. The prospect who says nothing nods politely and never calls you back. That's the one you should worry about.

When I was building Carroll Media, I learned to celebrate objections. Every time a prospect said, "Your price is too high," or "We're already working with someone," or "We need to think about it," I knew I was still in the game. I could work with that. The silent prospects who never engaged— they were already gone.

## The Five Most Common Objections (And How to Overcome Them)

In my experience across multiple businesses—from Yard Smart to Elite Fitness to Carroll Media—I've encountered virtually every objection you can imagine. However, most objections fall into five primary categories. Master these, and you'll be equipped to handle almost any resistance you encounter.

**1. Price Objections: "It's Too Expensive"**

The most common objection, "It's too expensive," rarely relates to actual price. When someone says your offering is "too expensive," what they're really saying is, "I don't see enough value to justify the investment."

How to Overcome It:

- Never Discount Immediately – The moment you drop your price, you confirm their suspicion that your offering wasn't worth what you initially asked. Instead, go back to value.

- Reframe the Investment – "I understand budget is a consideration. Let me ask: How much is it costing you to continue dealing with this problem?" Help them see the cost of not taking action.

- Break Down the Value - "When you look at what you're getting—[list specific benefits]—that's actually delivering tremendous value for the investment."

- Offer Payment Options - Sometimes, it's not the total price but the immediate cash outlay causing hesitation. "Would it be helpful to spread this investment over the next six months?"

Remember, a hunter doesn't lower the value of the kill—he helps the tribe understand why it's worth pursuing.

## 2. Timing Objections: "Let Me Think About It"

This objection is all about creating delay. It's not a firm "no," but it's not a "yes" either. It's the prospect of trying to create space to consider options or, more often, avoid making a decision.

How to Overcome It:

- Acknowledge the Need for Consideration - "I completely understand you want to make the right decision. This isn't something to rush into."

- Identify Specific Concerns - "So I can better address your questions when we next speak, may I ask what specific aspects you need to think about?"

- Create Urgency Through Scarcity - "We're currently booking projects for next month, and our calendar is filling quickly. I'd hate to see you miss that window."

- Schedule a Follow-Up - "Let's set a specific time to reconnect after you've had time to think. How about we touch base this Thursday at 2 PM?"

The hunter doesn't rush the kill but doesn't let the prey wander off, either. He maintains the engagement until the moment is right.

## 3. Authority Objections: "I Need to Check With..."

This objection appears when you're not talking to the final decision-maker. The prospect needs approval from someone else—a business partner, a spouse, a committee, or a boss.

How to Overcome It:

- <u>Identify All Decision-Makers Early</u> – "Before we go further, who else will be involved in making this decision?" This helps you address this objection before it even arises.

- <u>Ask to Include the Decision-Maker</u> – "Would it make sense to schedule a brief call with [the decision-maker] so I can address any questions they might have directly?"

- <u>Provide Materials to Share</u> – "I'm happy to provide information you can share with [the decision-maker]. What specific aspects would be most important for them to see?"

- <u>Set Expectations for Next Steps</u> – "After you speak with [the decision-maker], what would be our next step if they're on board? And if they have questions, how should we address those?"

The seasoned hunter knows that sometimes the prey isn't alone. You must be aware of the entire herd and how decisions are made.

## 4. Need Objections: "We Don't Need This Right Now"

This objection suggests that the prospect doesn't see how your offering addresses a pressing problem or desire. They don't see the urgency or necessity.

How to Overcome It:

- Revisit Pain Points – "Earlier, you mentioned that [specific challenge] was causing [specific negative impact]. Has that situation changed?"

- Create Future Regret – "Many of our clients initially felt the same way. What they found was that delaying cost them [specific consequence]. I'd hate to see that happen to you."

- Offer a Smaller Entry Point – "I understand. Many clients start with our [smaller offering] before moving to the full solution. Would that make more sense for your current situation?"

- Share Success Stories – "We recently worked with a client in a similar position. They were initially hesitant, but after implementing our solution, they saw [specific positive result]."

The hunter knows that prey doesn't always recognize the danger it's in. Sometimes, you have to help them see what they're missing.

## 5. Trust Objections: "We're Happy With Our Current Provider"

This objection is about loyalty and risk aversion. The prospect already has a solution, and switching to you feels risky. Why change what isn't broken?

How to Overcome It:

- <u>Acknowledge Their Loyalty</u> – "I respect that loyalty. It says something good about you and your provider: you've maintained that relationship."

- <u>Find the Gap</u> – "While you're generally happy with them, are there any areas where you wish they could improve? Even small things?"

- <u>Offer a Differential Value</u> – "What makes our approach unique is [specific differentiator]. Have they offered you anything similar?"

- <u>Suggest a Trial</u> – "I'm not asking you to switch providers completely. Would you be open to trying us for a small project so you can see the difference firsthand?"

The skilled hunter doesn't just chase any prey—he focuses on the ones who are slightly separated from the herd and showing signs of dissatisfaction or curiosity.

## The Psychology of Handling Rejection

Overcoming objections isn't just about technique—it's about mindset. It's about how you process and respond to the resistance you inevitably face.

### <u>Depersonalize the Rejection</u>

When someone says "no" to your offer, they're not saying "no" to you as a person. They're rejecting a specific proposition at a particular moment in time. The best salespeople—the true hunters—understand this distinction.

I've seen countless entrepreneurs take rejection personally. They hear "Your price is too high" and translate it to "You're not worth what you're asking." They hear "We're not interested" and translate it to "You're not interesting." This kind of personalization is deadly. It erodes confidence, kills motivation, and leads to burnout.

Instead, view objections as data points. They're valuable feedback that helps refine your approach, improve your offering, and enhance your hunting technique.

## Use Rejection as Fuel

The most successful entrepreneurs I know don't just tolerate rejection—they use it as fuel. Every "no" strengthens their resolve. Every objection makes them more determined to succeed.

When building my businesses, I developed a simple practice: After every rejection, I'd take a moment to acknowledge the sting. Then I'd ask myself: "What can I learn from this? How can I use this to get better?" I'd note the objection, refine my response, and move forward with renewed energy.

This practice transformed rejection from a setback into a stepping stone. It turned "no" into a necessary part of the journey to "yes."

## The Numbers Game Mindset

Success in sales and entrepreneurship is ultimately a numbers game. The more prospects you engage, the more objections you'll encounter, and the more sales you'll eventually close.

In my early days with Yard Smart, I set a goal of making 50 cold calls daily. Out of those 50 calls, I might get through to 20 people. Of those 20, perhaps 10 would engage in conversation. Of those 10, maybe five would agree to a quote. Of those 5, 2 or 3 might become customers.

Was it discouraging to face rejection 47 or 48 times a day? Initially, yes. But once I understood the numbers—once I saw that those rejections were simply part of the path to success—they lost their power over me. I started seeing objections as ?necessary steps in the process, not personal failures.

## Turning Objections Into Opportunities

The ultimate skill in handling objections is overcoming them and turning them into opportunities to strengthen your position and build deeper trust.

### The Feel-Felt-Found Method

One of the most powerful techniques I've used throughout my career is the Feel-Felt-Found method. I learned this from one of my first mentors Ken Fenner; It's a simple three-step process that acknowledges the objection, normalizes it, and then reframes it:

- **Feel** - "I understand how you feel. That's a legitimate concern."
- **Felt** - "Many of our clients felt the same way before working with us."
- **Found** - "What they found after action was [specific positive outcome]."

This approach shows empathy, builds connection and provides social proof—all within a few sentences. It's remarkably effective because it doesn't invalidate the prospect's concern; it simply puts it in a context where it can be addressed.

### The Objection Loop

Another powerful technique is what I call the "Objection Loop." Instead of immediately presenting a counter-argument, you ask clarifying questions that help both you and the prospect better understand the real issue:

1. <u>Acknowledge the objection</u> – "I appreciate you sharing that concern."

2. <u>Ask for clarification</u> – "To make sure I understand, what specifically about [the timing/price/etc.] is causing hesitation?"

3. <u>Listen deeply</u> – Pay attention not just to the words but to the underlying concerns.

4. <u>Respond to the root cause</u> – Address the real issue, not just the surface objection.

5. <u>Confirm resolution</u> – "Does that address your concern, or is there something else you're thinking about?"

This loop ensures you're solving the right problem, not just the stated objection. Often, the first objection is masking a deeper concern that the prospect may not even be consciously aware of.

## The Hunter's Advantage: Preparation Beats Objections

The best way to handle objections is to prevent them from arising in the first place. This doesn't mean you'll never face resistance—that's inevitable in the hunt. But by anticipating objections and addressing them proactively, you can significantly reduce their impact.

### The Pre-emptive Strike

Before an objection can even form in the prospect's mind, address it directly:

- **For price objections** – "You might be wondering about the investment. What makes our solution different is the return you'll see within the first 90 days..."
- **For timing objections** – "Many clients initially think they should wait before implementing this. They discover that every month of delay is costing them..."
- **For trust objections** – "I know you may already be working with someone. We're not asking you to replace them entirely. We're simply offering a new approach to complement your already doing..."

You demonstrate confidence and control the narrative by bringing potential objections into the open and addressing them on your terms.

### The Objection Inventory

One practice that transformed my sales approach was creating an "Objection Inventory"—a comprehensive list of every objection I'd ever encountered and the most effective responses.

After each sales conversation, I'd add any new objections to the list and refine my responses based on what worked and what didn't. Over time, this inventory became an invaluable resource that prepared me for virtually any resistance.

I recommend creating your own Objection Inventory. Start with the five common categories I outlined earlier, then add specific objections you encounter in your business. Review and update this inventory regularly. The more prepared you are, the more confidently you'll handle objections when they arise.

## The Ultimate Mindset: Objections Are Steps to Yes

The most profound shift in my career came when I stopped seeing objections as obstacles and started seeing them as steps. Each objection addressed, each concern resolved, is a step closer to "yes."

Think about it: If a prospect has no objections, one of two things is happening—either they're already completely sold (rare) or not engaged enough to raise concerns (common). The engaged prospect asks questions. They raise concerns. They need reassurance. And each time you provide that reassurance, you build trust and move them closer to the sale.

The hunter understands that the path to the kill isn't always straight. There are detours, obstacles, and moments of uncertainty. However, overcoming each challenge makes the final success more meaningful and profitable.

## Embrace the No

Early in my career, I was terrified of rejection. Each "no" felt like a personal failure, a judgment on my worth as a salesperson and a human being. I would avoid making calls, delay follow-ups, and find excuses not to engage prospects who seemed likely to object.

The turning point came when a mentor challenged me to collect 100 "no's" weekly. Not sales—rejections. He wanted me to fill a notebook with objections and rejections. At first, I thought he was crazy. Why would I actively seek rejection?

But the magic of this exercise was that it completely changed my relationship with the word "no." Suddenly, rejection wasn't something to fear—it was something to pursue, collect, and study. Each "no" became valuable data, not a personal affront.

Something unexpected happened along the way: I started making sales in my quest for 100 rejections—lots of them. Because I was no longer afraid of objections, I became more confident, persistent, and paradoxically, more successful.

That lesson has stayed with me throughout my entrepreneurial journey. I've learned to embrace rejection, to see objections as opportunities, and to recognize that the road to "yes" is often paved with a series of "no's."

## The Hunter's Creed: Rejection Is the Path

As we close this section, I want to leave you with what I call the Hunter's Creed when it comes to objections and rejection:

1. **Seek rejection actively** - The more "no's" you collect, the closer you get to "yes."
2. **Depersonalize every "no"** - It's not about you; it's about timing, the fit, and the circumstances.
3. **Learn from every objection** - Each makes you stronger, smarter, and more effective.
4. **Prepare relentlessly** - Anticipate objections before they arise.
5. **Value persistence over perfection** - The hunter who keeps tracking eventually makes the kill.

Rejection isn't just something to overcome—it's the very path to success. It's the crucible that forges entrepreneurs. It's the test that separates the hunters from the hunted.

And here's the ultimate truth: The only way to avoid rejection entirely is never to take a shot. But the hunter who never takes a shot, never eats. The entrepreneur who never faces objections never closes a deal. A business that never encounters resistance will never grow.

So, embrace the objections. Welcome the "no's." See them not as roadblocks but as necessary steps on your journey to success. Because in the end, it's not about avoiding rejection—it's about persisting through it until you reach your goal.

And remember: You're not truly in business until you've been rejected. You're not really in sales until you've heard "no" more times than you can count. And you're not a hunter until you've tracked prey that initially tried to flee.

The hunt continues. The objections will come. And when they do, you'll be ready to overcome them and use them as fuel for your ultimate success.

# CHAPTER 5

# Stacking Skulls: Tactical Execution

*The feast comes not from a single spear thrust, but a thousand silent steps.*

*The hunter leaves the camp at dawn. Each day. No glory in yesterday's kill. There is no rest today.*

*The hunter who boasts of past conquests while skipping daily rituals soon starves. Mastery lives in repetition—hand moving without thought, eye seeing what others miss, mind anticipating without strain.*

*The weak chase the magnificent leap. The wise build the unbreakable pattern.*

*Discipline. Choice. Refusal to surrender to "tomorrow." Actual predators know power lies not in intention but in execution.*

*Time—the most precious prey—cannot be stored, borrowed, or recovered once gone. Master time, master all.*

*Will you chase shadows today? Or stalk the daily kill with precision, knowing - greatness dwells not on mountaintops but in valleys of consistent action.*

*The daily kill feeds both body and spirit. Conquer each day, conquer life.*

# The Power of Micro-Goals in Business Growth

In the world of hunters, a critical truth separates those who feast from those who starve: The hunt doesn't end with one kill. Every day brings a new need to track, pursue, and capture. The most successful hunters aren't just focused on the big game—they're skilled at securing a steady stream of smaller prey that keeps the tribe fed between major hunts.

## The Daily Kill

Learning to set goals correctly created a sense of self-accountability that was missing from my life early on. Everyone understands the basic premise of goals. It's about picking a destination you want to get to. But I didn't realize that balancing your goals is the only way to keep yourself balanced. This ensures that you are working on all areas of your life.

I remember starting my first business and thinking, "If I can get to $100,000 in sales, I'll have made it." What escaped me was the sacrifices I made in other areas of my life. I'm not talking about partying and girls but about relationships, health, surroundings, and mental well-being. I was grinding my gears 20+ hours a day chasing that number that I had placed so much value on. It wasn't worth it.

If I could give you a word of advice, take care of your body and mind first. Stay sharp by exercising and learning. My hustle has changed over time as I learned to set goals properly. Now, I look for the roadblocks that may be coming, what I can do to avoid them, who I can hire, and what I can read. I've learned that being rich and ill serves no one. But by becoming clear on your goals, you can achieve your version of a happy life.

# Focusing on Today's Kill

Today is the only thing you need to focus on. What are you going to hunt down today? If you focus 100% of your energy on taking massive amounts of action on a micro-day-to-day level, your long-term macro success is unavoidable.

This book is about hunting in business, but I will tell you exactly how I built my first business. Day in and day out, I would force myself to make 100 dials. The result: I landed my three biggest clients from those calls. This reveals the power of persistence and focusing on winning the day, which is precisely what it takes.

Concentrating on winning the day will push you on the proper track to win the week; when you win the week, you win the month, and so on. The problem with most entrepreneurs is that they get so consumed with the big picture and talking about the big game that they forget to play the game of the day. You don't have to hit a home run every day. Hell, you don't even have to win every day. But please, for the sake of all things entrepreneurial - please get up, get dressed, and get out the door!

# Tracking Your Hunt

I didn't know what I could accomplish in a day until I started tracking my progress towards my goals. By charting down precisely what I was doing every hour of every day, I quickly realized that I was wasting a shit load of time. I wasn't focused on achieving my goals mainly because I hadn't tracked my activities.

You are in for a treat if you have never set a goal. Once you write that objective on paper, your entire day is either spent working towards it or pulling you further away. There is no treading water in business, in sales, or hunting. You either make progress towards a kill, or you don't. The best part is there is no one to blame but yourself.

Some people end up closing shops because they weren't aware of it or didn't like the constant pressure to perform. I wasn't joking when I said you are taking your life into your own hands - but if you aren't fearful of your potential, this should excite you more than it scares you.

## Micro-Goals In Action

In 2013, I was hired to perform a full training day with two full-time salespeople at an insurance office. After meeting with the owner that morning, he informed us that they needed to get one of their product lines up by the end of the year. Mind you, this was in October. I had my work cut out for me, to say the least.

Before training, I needed to get the entire team focused on the objective. We needed to focus on getting this product line in front of every client who walked through the door. I needed this to stay at the top of their minds. Sometimes, the best systems are the simplest. I went into the break room and wrote on two separate sticky notes the following:

"Sales to date XXX Goal by Dec 31st XXX."

I took those notes and taped them to the monitor on each desk. The mind will achieve that it is continually reminded to attract. We spent the rest of the day working on tactics we could use to close more deals in said product line.

I followed up with the client mid-way through January of the following year. He was happy to report that they sold more of that product line in the 4th quarter than in the previous three COMBINED! I'd like to say this was due to my training, and maybe it partially was, but I believe that setting a goal, committing to it, and keeping it in front of them was the real game changer. Goals work - but they aren't something you write about once a year and then shelf off for the remaining months.

## The Activity Monitoring System

I have a system called the Activity Monitoring Sheet (AMS). This sheet is the protocol I used to grow my company from a $300 start-up to over $3 million in revenue. You can't possibly know how you are doing regarding tracking your goals unless you track your activities.

Here are my main activities to track:

- Dials/Touches - Outbound Calls or Cold DM's (direct messages) on Facebook, LinkedIn, Twitter, or Instagram.
- Significant Conversations - Anything other than a "He's not here," "No Thanks," or "Click"
- Appointments Set - Qualifying phone calls or messages
- Deals Pitched - Presentation made to qualified prospects in person or via the web
- Deals Closed - Number of 100% closed, signed, and delivered deals
- Referrals Request - This would be an email or voicemail drop requesting a referral from a past client
- Old Client Touches - Messages or calls to past clients

Tracking your progress day in and day out will not only keep you from being surprised by an empty bank account at the end of the month but will significantly help build your confidence and help you keep yourself accountable.

## Understanding Timelines

The most difficult part of this entire goal-setting process is understanding timelines. Every business has its own unique journey, and reality rarely matches our initial plans. That's how the game is played. You must be able to audible. You can't fall in love with the goals you wrote on paper. Doing so will cripple you. Timelines will change - your job is to ebb and flow with the market's movement.

## Your Commitment to the Hunt

Remember what my cross country coach in high school would always tell us during practice - if you want to quit, go ahead; you aren't giving up on me; you're giving up on you. The same is true about setting goals. There is something magical that happens when you make a commitment to yourself and then follow through.

When I coach clients, I put them through an extensive application process. I can sniff out a quitter from a mile away and have no interest in pouring my time or resources into it. If you are going to succeed in life, you need to learn to set goals and hold YOURSELF accountable to those goals. Take charge of your life in all areas. Leave nothing to chance.

## Your Mental Canvas

Your life is a paint-by-numbers canvas located between your ears. Every morning, you should wake up excited to be alive, hydrate your body, and then start with a review of your mental canvas. Closing your eyes and seeing exactly what you want your life to look like. You can't expect much from your life if you never take the time to design it.

As you see the whole picture, don't forget to admire what you have already finished. The colors are already on the canvas. Feel a sense of happiness and gratitude for the life that you have lived this far. Then, focus on the piece of the picture you will work on today. Make a note and take action. Feel free to revisit your mental canvas throughout the day. When life gets stressful, take a time out, focus on your breath, and close your eyes. Look at the amazing color you have already painted and find that sense of gratitude.

## Setting Your Sights

The best time to plant a tree was 20 years ago; the second best is today. No matter how great or terrible your past is-- it's the past. You must focus on your forward vision starting today. That means making goals a part of the rest of your life.

I always like to set my goals for the upcoming year during the break around Thanksgiving in the US. This 5-day window (the day before Thanksgiving and the 3 days following it) is the perfect time for me to reflect on everything I am thankful for and focus on the things left to accomplish. I like to break my goals into five categories: Finance, Relationship, Environment, Spirituality, and Health & Fitness.

I break my yearly goals into quarterly goals. I do the same for each of my companies. I fill out the 1-page goal action planner for each goal, which is a pretty significant undertaking, and that is why I give myself a decent window of time to accomplish it.

Nothing great ever just shows up and knocks on your door. It takes planning and action to achieve the high levels of success that most entrepreneurs desire. Get the complete goal action planner by going to TheHunterHeadGame.com.

Like the hunter who prepares for the daily kill rather than waiting for the rare big game, your consistent micro-goal execution will determine your entrepreneurial survival and success. The hunt begins now, hunter. One small kill at a time.

Let's turn to the critical skills that makes your micro-goals achievable: the strategic management of your most precious and finite resource—time.

# Time Maximization and Daily Routines for Success

Time is the kill shot.

It's not money. It's not talent. It's not an opportunity. Every hunter is issued the same weapon at the start of each day: 24 hours. What separates the apex from the average isn't what they're given—it's how precise they become with their aim.

When I talk about time, I'm not talking about calendars and clocks. I'm talking about dominance. Control. Ownership of your minutes, like your life depends on it—because it does.

Most people aren't lazy. They're just unfocused. They're distracted, hunted by chaos, and reacting to every ring, ding, and ping-like prey flinching at every sound in the woods. Hunters don't flinch. They stalk. They move deliberately. They kill with intention.

When building my companies, I learned quickly that if I didn't put a grip on my day, it would run me. I'd wake up in the whirlwind—emails, team fires, client issues, unread texts, 37 Slack pings, and maybe one or two "emergencies" that weren't emergencies. If you've lived it, you know that's not a business. That's a zoo.

So, I built a system.

You may have heard me talk about *Time Max*—a philosophy, a system, and honestly, a lifestyle. The framework took me from being reactive and scattered to operating like a tactical weapon. It's how I built a multi-million dollar business while keeping my sanity intact.

Let's break it down.

## Start With the Apex Hour

Everyone I've ever met who dominates their industry has one thing in common: they own their first hour of the day.

No scroll. No snooze. No chaos.

That first hour is where you sharpen the blade. For me, it's early. I'm up at 4:30 AM. Why? Because the world is quiet. Nobody needs me yet. I haven't been pulled in a thousand directions. It's just me and the mission.

Here's what I do:

- **Mindset Reset** – Before anything, I journal or meditate. Not because it's a trend, but because clarity is currency. If I don't reset my mind, I carry yesterday's crap into today's strategy.

- **Movement** – I get my body going. Maybe it's weights, maybe it's cardio. Doesn't matter. A static body leads to a sluggish mind.

- **Mission Review** – I review my "Big 3" daily goals. These aren't random to-dos. These are the top 3 outcomes that push the needle—the kill shots.

You don't have to copy my hour. You just have to *claim* yours.

## Plan Your Day Like a Military Operation

If you looked at my calendar, you'd think I was planning an invasion. That's how tight it is. Every block is spoken for. Not because I like being rigid—but because the battlefield demands structure.

Inside *Time Max*, one of my online courses, I teach people to run their day using "Focus Blocks." It's a simple method, but deadly effective.

- **Focus Block (90 mins):** Deep work. No distractions. Phone off. Emails closed. This is where I crush big things—content creation, vision planning, critical meetings.

- **Flex Block (60 mins):** Reactive time. Responding to emails, checking in with the team, and handling quick tasks.

- **Admin Block (30 mins):** Back-end stuff—approvals, finance, CRM updates. Keep it short and clean.

- **Recharge Block (variable):** Walks. Food. Breath. Reset your energy so you can come back sharp.

Every block has a purpose. If your calendar is just a list of meetings, you're not leading—you're surviving. You have to zoom out and ask, "Does this schedule reflect a hunter or a herded sheep?"

## Kill the Chaos With a Preloaded Week

If you're planning your day *during* your day, you've already lost.

The *real one's* plan *in advance*. My Sundays are sacred. That's when I preload the week.

What does that mean? I go into my calendar and block time for the things that matter before the chaos can fill the cracks. I literally put in time for family, sales calls, content, team development, and workouts—*before* the world gets a chance to book me. I look at my Big 3 – business goals, health, & relationships, then reverse engineer the week. I ask, "If I were a sniper, what are the three kills I need to take this week to move my mission forward?"

Most people build their week around availability. Hunters build it around *intent*.

## Eliminate, Delegate, Dominate

The hunter doesn't do everything in the village.

He doesn't mend the nets. He doesn't count the grain. He doesn't sharpen every spear.

He hunts.

If you want to operate like an apex predator, you must eliminate, delegate, and dominate.

- **Eliminate**: Cut the noise. It doesn't belong on your plate if it doesn't move the needle. "Nice to have" is code for "Never gonna matter."

- **Delegate**: Hand it off. Your genius is wasted on $20/hour tasks. If someone else can do it 80% as well as you, pass the torch.

- **Dominate**: This is where your zone of genius lives. The strategy. The relationships. The revenue-producing moves. This is your weapon. Wield it.

Time maximization isn't about doing more. It's about doing less, but doing it with *lethal precision*.

## The Hunter's Weekly Review

Here's the part nobody talks about: even apex predators need feedback loops.

Every Friday, I run a personal after-action review. 20 minutes. That's it.

I ask myself:

- What did I kill this week?
- What hunted me?
- What needs to change?

Journaling is an exercise that helps you become more deadly. With every week's test, you either advance, or die with your excuses.

## Your Time Is a Weapon

You're not looking for theory if you've made it this far into the book. You're looking for execution. Here's the truth:

> "Your calendar is your scoreboard. Your habits are your hunting ground. Your time is your most violent weapon."

I've trained entrepreneurs, agents, investors, creators—and the common thread isn't talent. It's discipline. It's repetition. It's the ability to wake up every day and hunt with focus.

If you master time, you master the game.

And if you don't, you will always be hunted by those who do.

# Overcoming Procrastination and Staying Disciplined

Let's just call it what it is—procrastination is self-betrayal in disguise.

It's not a scheduling problem. It's not about laziness. It's not about needing more reminders, planners, or another app that pings your wrist every hour. No—procrastination happens when the vision isn't clear, the cost isn't real, and the identity isn't locked in.

Because when you *know* who you are—and what you're hunting—you don't need motivation. You need a map.

Here's the truth: discipline doesn't come from reading motivational quotes or listening to another podcast. Discipline is built in the dark. It's forged when nobody's watching, the results haven't shown up yet, and the payoff still feels like a rumor.

And I get it—procrastination feels safe. It gives you an out. It whispers, *"You'll do it tomorrow. You'll feel more ready next week."* But let me be the one to tell you there is no version of your future where you feel *more ready* than you do right now.

Procrastination is a liar. It's a thief dressed in comfort. And it's stealing your shot.

## The Discipline Shift

Discipline isn't about perfection—it's about identity.

If you see yourself as someone who gets things done, discipline becomes automatic. It's not a battle of willpower every morning. It's not a question of "Should I?"—it becomes "This is just what I do."

You don't brush your teeth because you're feeling inspired. You brush your teeth because you're the person who brushes them. Same with sending that follow-up. Same with making that call. It's the same with knocking out that content, dialing that lead, building that system, and training your people.

Discipline becomes the default when your identity shifts from "someone trying" to "someone becoming."

## The Identity Lock-In Exercise

If procrastination is the enemy of progress, identity is the antidote.

So, here's something I challenge every one of my clients and team members to do:

Write down your Apex Identity. Not who you are now—but who you are becoming in the present tense.

---

> *"I am a disciplined operator who handles the hard things first."*
> *"I execute daily, even when it's uncomfortable."*
> *"I finish what I start. I do what I say I'm going to do."*

---

This isn't some fluffy affirmation—this is how the hunter rewires his software. You can't build the Apex version of yourself based on yesterday's mindset. You must upgrade your internal script. Daily.

Tape it to your mirror. Set it as your lock screen. Read it before every work block. Let that identity override the old voice that says, "Not today."

## Discipline Is a Decision

People treat discipline like it's a personality trait—you either have it or you don't. Wrong. Discipline is a decision you make repeatedly until it becomes second nature.

And if I can be real with you for a second—some of you are losing because you're still deciding how you *feel* about the work. You're checking your energy, vibe, inbox, and horoscope—but you're not checking your commitment.

You know who doesn't negotiate with themselves every morning? A disciplined hunter.

He wakes up, loads the weapon, and gets after it. Because he's not reacting to feelings—he's following orders. Orders he gave himself when he was clear, focused, and committed.

## The Pain of the Unlived Life

Do you want to kill procrastination? Stop fantasizing about future rewards and start getting intimate with future regrets.

Visualize what it'll feel like to have wasted the next 5 years. To have let your family down. Still spinning in the same cycle of good ideas and no results. Let that sink in—not to punish yourself, but to wake yourself up.

Urgency doesn't come from hype. It comes from clarity. From realizing that time isn't a renewable resource—and you're burning daylight.

# Tactics That Work (When the Motivation Doesn't)

Let's make this practical. Here's how I coach my team and clients by staying disciplined even when the wheels are coming off:

1. **The Rule of One**
   Every day, pick the *one* task that, if completed, would move the needle forward. That's your non-negotiable. You don't end the day without it done.

2. **Use Deadlines Like Weapons**
   Deadlines don't create stress—they create action. Assign due dates. Publicly, if possible. Use pressure in your favor.

3. **Start Before You're Ready**
   Waiting for the perfect time? Let me save you some time: there is none. Progress begins with movement, not mastery.

4. **Micro Wins, Macro Vision**
   You don't build an empire in a weekend. But you can stack 20 minutes of focused execution today. Do that enough, and suddenly, you're dangerous.

5. **Default to Action**
   When in doubt, move. Hunters don't sit in indecision. Action creates clarity. Waiting creates rust.

## Burn the Old Script

Look—every excuse you've ever told yourself? Burn it. The story about why you're not ready, why it's too hard, why someone else has it easier? Trash it.

You don't need more time. You need more clarity. You don't need more inspiration. You need a better identity. You don't need to wait for the stars to align. You need to decide that *you are done playing small.*

Let the world be shocked by your consistency. Let your hunger inspire your family. Let your legacy be built brick by brick—on the back of your discipline.

You're not fighting procrastination. You're fighting for your Apex.

And you're sharpening the blade every time you act when it would've been easier to stall. You're separating from the herd. You're stepping into the version of you that your future depends on.

> *In the hunter's journey, there comes a moment of profound truth: mindset alone will not feed the tribe.*

It is crucial to transition from thinking like a hunter to acting like one.

The difference between the entrepreneur who starves and the one who feasts isn't found in grand visions or motivational quotes—it's in the relentless execution of daily action. The Daily Kill is where theory meets practice, where intention transforms into impact.

We've explored the hunter's mentality. We've uncovered the strengths that make you dangerous. Now, we confront the battlefield where most entrepreneurs falter: tactical execution. Because in business, as in the hunt, glory doesn't come from what you know or dream—it comes from what you do consistently when no one is watching.

This chapter reveals the weapons of daily execution: micro-goals that build unstoppable momentum, time maximization systems that eliminate chaos, and disciplined routines that turn procrastination into productivity. These aren't just strategies but survival tools for the modern business hunter.

The harsh reality? Your competition doesn't care about your potential. The market doesn't reward your intentions. Only results matter, and results come from relentless, tactical execution.

As you master The Daily Kill, you'll discover that greatness isn't born in moments of inspiration but in the mundane moments of consistent action. The entrepreneur who wins isn't always the smartest or the most connected—it's the one who shows up daily, executes ruthlessly, and refuses to be outworked.

This is where hunters are separated from the hunted. This is where talking ends and doing begins. This is where your legacy is forged—one daily kill at a time.

The question is no longer, "Do you think like a hunter?" The question is now, "Will you hunt today?"

# CHAPTER 6

# Carnivore Camaraderie: The Power of Association

*Behold the great truth written in the blood of generations: No hunter walks the path of greatness alone.*

*In the time before memory, when the first hunters ventured forth, it was decreed that strength would flow not from solitude but from unity. For lo, it is written in the ancient code of predators: as iron sharpens iron, so one hunter sharpens another.*

*The lion does not teach its young to graze among lambs. She surrounds them with other lions, so they might learn to roar before facing the unforgiving wilderness.*

*Heed this warning: a hunter who keeps company with prey soon loses his appetite for the kill. His claws grow dull, his senses dim, and his spirit weakens under the weight of lesser ambitions.*

*The sacred covenant of the pack remains unbroken through ages: your circle becomes your ceiling, your companions become your limitations, and your fellowship becomes your future.*

*When the mighty hunter seeks worthy allies, many will present themselves. Few will prove worthy. Discernment separates those who merely walk beside you from those who truly walk with you.*

*Some companions must remain behind so that others might be found ahead. This is the hard wisdom of the ascending path, that not all who begin the journey will complete. So, with whom do you hunt?*

# The Law of Association: You Are Who You Surround Yourself With

If you have read any personal development book, you may have heard of the "Law of Association," which means, <u>*You are the sum of the five people you are around the most*</u>. Suppose your five closest associates are criminals; your likelihood of being a criminal increases. If your five closest associates are lazy and procrastinate, your likelihood of being lazy and procrastinating increases. You will most likely do the same if your five closest associates are engaged in continuous gossiping and negativity.

Look closely at the five people you spend the most time with. Examine their income levels, their health habits, their mindsets, their ambitions, and their energy. Now look in the mirror. Uncomfortable, isn't it? The truth often is. You are becoming the average of those five people—financially, physically, mentally, and spiritually. This isn't a coincidence. It's causation.

In the business world, I quickly realized the size and type of opportunities I encountered were because of my associations. If I hung around people who were movers and shakers, it seemed as if something new was always in the works. Reflect on when you hang with "friends." Do you find yourself talking, acting, and thinking like them in a very short time? I quickly noticed this in my words and actions around the people I associated with. I began to speak and behave similarly. The law of association essentially says you conform to the likes of those around you.

I propose reframing the "Law of Association" to the "Power of Association." Why? Because of its universal power. When you truly understand and apply this principle, it becomes one of the most transformative forces in your entrepreneurial journey.

## Rating Your Current Pack

I want to give you a way to rate your current pack. First and foremost, you must ensure your values are aligned. Do your friends care about what will make you highly successful in the long term in business? Integrity, Honor, and Legacy are the main pillars of a successful person. Do your friends display these traits?

I've found it easy to associate with other hunters. Let me clarify that hunters don't necessarily have to be business owners. One of my pack members is a local Toyota store's new car sales manager. He has dreams of learning and earning enough to open his own Toyota store one day. This guy is a hunter. Rating your current pack could be as easy as deciding who has it in them and who doesn't. At the very least, take a conscious tally of who you let in your life.

As growth-oriented, I encourage you to adopt the same strengths-based mentality to achieve your ultimate goals. Place yourself in a room among people who are more intelligent and more successful than you. If that's not happening, then find a different room. Find different friends. I know this is difficult, leading you to ask, "But DJ, I have been friends with this person for 10 years."

Look, I get it. It's not an easy choice to change the people around you because of your history. But what if this choice was a matter of life or death? I told you this book would have some pretty offensive stuff, so here's the harsh reality: 90 percent of the people you define as your friends really don't care about you, your success, or your dreams. They don't care because they don't understand, which is evident when many of those "friends" consider you lame or boring when you skip the club to work on your business systems or finish a proposal. This lack of support is a tell-tale sign of what they genuinely believe about you.

## Never Tolerate A Lack of Appetite

As hunters, our success is determined not just by our own hunger but by the appetite of those we surround ourselves with. At the risk of repeating myself - I'll say again - If you tolerate a lack of appetite in your circle, it will eventually dull your own edge. That's why one of the hardest but most necessary decisions you'll ever make is auditing your relationships and cutting ties with those who lack hunger.

I call these people "energy vampires"—they leave you feeling depleted, discouraged, and diminished after interactions. They're the ones who respond to your business ideas with "that will never work" rather than "how can I help?" They're the ones who subtly celebrate your failures and minimize your victories.

The most dangerous energy vampires aren't strangers—they're often family members, long-term friends, or relatives whose influence has become so normalized you can't see it clearly. Their cynicism masquerades as "being realistic." Their fear disguises itself as "looking out for you." Their complacency presents as "being content."

This isn't always because they wish you ill. Often, it's because they genuinely care but lack the vision or courage to understand your path. Their concern manifests as doubt, their protection as limitation, their love as fear. They're operating from their own framework of what's possible and safe, not yours.

## Pride In Your Pride

Pride is the special sauce that creates confidence. Spread that around an entire group of comrades, and you will have the makings of something great. I don't think enough people have pride in the company they keep. It's probably why many people let riff-raff into their life without checking it. You need to be proud of every single one of your friends. Life is way too short to keep garbage around. Yet that is precisely what most of us do.

It's not until they betray you that you realize they were only along for the ride because you were giving them something they wanted. Not being proud of my circle cost me almost $10,000 once. A good friend had fallen on tough times and approached me about a job. I felt obligated, so I caved. Unfortunately, he stole over $4,000 in cash, costing me several opportunities that added up to several thousand more.

I've never done a huge rebuild of my circle because it's always an ongoing progressive move as you reach new levels of success. As you set new goals for yourself, some people in your circle will naturally fall off because they aren't growing as fast as you are. That's OK, and you can't make yourself feel bad about it. We only have a finite number of years on this planet. We can't dillydally around, worrying about hurting people's feelings or what others may think of us. Be unapologetically yourself and never apologize for having big goals.

When you find yourself surrounded by people who doubt your vision, question your plans, or find entertainment in your setbacks, it's time to create distance. Their negativity isn't just neutral—it actively weighs you down and creates friction against your efforts.

As you grow and evolve, it's essential to regularly audit your circle. Ask yourself: Who inspires me? Who drains me? Who am I becoming because of my circle? The answers to these questions might be uncomfortable, but they're necessary for your growth as a hunter.

# Finding the Right Mentors and Business Allies

Early in my journey to entrepreneurship, I was fortunate to find mentors to help guide me along the way. My first mentor, Mark Smith, was my insurance agent. We met for breakfast at a riverside diner in Carrollton called Welches—a hole in the wall place by the river—every other week to discuss business tactics and ideas. These weren't fancy strategy sessions with PowerPoints and spreadsheets. They were simple conversations over breakfast and coffee about the fundamental building blocks of business.

Mark taught me principles that seem obvious in hindsight but were transformative for a young entrepreneur: do what you say you're going to do when you say you're going to do it; show up when you say you're going to show up; over-deliver instead of over-promising. It was super helpful because every couple of weeks I had a sounding board that I could debrief with about my current struggles. Since Mark had been in business for so long, he could easily tell me stories or paint pictures that would help me better understand what I needed to do.

This guy cut decades off my learning curve. Having someone to bounce ideas off is invaluable; finding that mentor is easier than you might think. Mentors are all around you.

## Choosing the Right Mentor

I challenge you to courageously reach out to a successful person you admire for their business acumen and mentorship. This could be someone you know in town or someone on the other side of the world on social media. With the many technological advances of our generation, it's never been easier to contact someone you look up to. Seriously, go to your choice of social media platform, message a successful business person you admire, and ask them to mentor you.

You'd be surprised to find out who will respond and help you out.

Over the years, I have learned to hunt from many of my mentors. Some taught me the slower relationship type of selling. Others taught me how to cold call and be a Closer. One taught me the ideology of tiered pricing and how to sell in packages that would increase profit. I learned from books, mainly audiobooks because I am mildly dyslexic. After a full day, I learned lessons from YouTube videos late at night. Actually, YouTube is where I found the mentor who taught me the most tools about selling, including the psychology behind it and how to persuade people to take action to buy when I knew they wouldn't otherwise.

## The 10X Mentor Principle

As your business grows, you should continually seek mentors who are at least 10 times more accomplished than you. I call this the 10X Mentor Principle, inspired by Grant Cardone, who has been an incredible mentor to me throughout my entrepreneurial journey. Grant's philosophy of thinking and acting at 10X levels revolutionized how I approach both business growth and personal development.

Why 10X? Because someone operating at 10X your level has encountered and solved problems you haven't even imagined yet. They see opportunities invisible to you. Their standards force you to elevate your thinking.

This doesn't mean you need to find a billionaire if you're making $100,000. It means finding someone who has achieved what you're striving for and is significantly further along the path. If you have 5 employees, find someone with 50. If you have 2 locations, connect with someone who has 20.

The 10X mentor will challenge your thinking, expand your vision, and help you see beyond your current constraints. Their advice might sometimes seem impractical or overwhelming because they're operating at a different level. But that stretching is precisely what you need to break through your mental barriers.

Grant Cardone taught me that most people massively underestimate what they're capable of achieving, largely because they're surrounded by conventional thinking. By connecting with mentors operating at 10X levels, you recalibrate your sense of what's possible.

## The Ladder of Success

The ladder of success is the never-ending pursuit of finding better mentors and comrades in your journey through life. This fictional ladder has no top. The purpose is to focus on learning everything you can as you climb. The people, experience, and losses all have lessons. As you climb, you will fall, so don't let that discourage you. People you thought you could trust will mislead you; don't let that discourage you. You will make money, and you will lose money.

As you climb, learn to love the stage that you are on. You only get to do this thing called life one time. The experiences only come once. I'll never forget the first keynote I gave. I had a grown man come up to me, crying afterward. That's when I learned that I must appreciate and be grateful throughout this journey. You will have those experiences as well. Don't get so focused on climbing to the top of the ladder of success that you never see the view as you climb.

Herb Kinman was a great mentor I had who passed away 3 years after I met him. He owned several local dealerships and a lot of real estate. The guy was a straight HUSTLER! I know there were billions of dollars to be learned in lessons from that man - but because I was young - I was more focused on the money than the knowledge I could have gained from him. So, after picking him up as a landscaping client - I'd really only talk to him when I picked up the monthly bill or came into the store to use the bathroom while onsite working. This was a guy I should have been taking to dinner once a month. I promise everything you want to achieve is possible. It is going to take making the right moves at the right time. Don't let your ambition cause you to fall. Learn to be patient - it's not easy, but it will allow you to gain perspective.

## Swimming With Sharks

Have you heard the saying, "Swim with fish and you'll be eaten by sharks?" What if you could swim with the sharks without being a shark? That's exactly what pilot fish do. That's what you must do.

Pilot fish are small fish that have a symbiotic relationship with sharks, particularly the whitetip reef shark. These little fish swim alongside predators, eating parasites off the sharks and feeding on the leftovers from the sharks' meals. The sharks get cleaned, and the pilot fish get fed—mutualism at its finest.

Don't be afraid to be around people more successful than you. This is a huge mistake I see many early-stage entrepreneurs make. You can't make it on your own. If you are going to make it past the 60-month mark, you have to find people who hunt for the same clients as you, but service them differently.

Just like how the pilot fish survives by feeding off the parasites and leftovers of the whitetip reef shark, you, too, can swim with sharks in the early stages of your business and survive by creating mutualism in the market. Mutualism in the market saves you tremendously in the tough times.

I've experienced this firsthand with Rod and some of the old guards from the apartment association. I would go to networking events with them, hang out at the bar afterward or during cocktail hour, and be the pilot fish—just sitting in the background, waiting for them to say, "Oh, by the way, do you know DJ?" and make the introduction to their bigger circle of sharks.

Rod met me at my very first trade show—he was just super friendly and helpful. He came over to the booth and introduced himself, told me what he did, and as a young 20-something-year-old kid, he could tell that I was wet behind the ears and very green to the industry. He didn't lose anything or gain anything by helping me out at that first trade show, but he did it because it was the right thing to do.

After that first interaction at the trade show, Rod became a great friend and colleague, and we have exchanged referrals for over a decade. I'll go years without talking to him now and get a random text that says, "Hey, DJ, so-and-so at such-and-such property could use your services. Here's her information. I told her you'd reach out."

## Creating Strategic Business Alliances

Creating strategic business alliances is one of the most powerful ways to accelerate your growth as a hunter. These are different from mentorships—they're peer relationships based on mutual benefit rather than guidance. The right business allies can open doors, extend your reach, and provide critical support when challenges arise.

When seeking business allies, look for these qualities:

- **Complementary offerings**: They serve the same clients but offer different services
- **Shared values**: Their approach to business ethics aligns with yours
- **Mutual respect**: They recognize your value just as you recognize theirs
- **Reliable follow-through**: They do what they say they'll do

- **Natural rapport**: There's an easy chemistry that makes collaboration enjoyable

Business alliances don't need to be formalized with contracts and agreements (though sometimes that makes sense). Often, the most powerful alliances develop organically through consistent mutual support over time.

The key is to approach these relationships with a genuine desire to give value, not just extract it. Ask yourself: "How can I help this person succeed?" rather than "What can this person do for me?" When you lead with generosity, reciprocity often follows naturally.

# The Benefits of Networking and Collaboration

The right relationships don't just shape who you are—they determine what you can accomplish. Creating a pack to hunt with could be one of your most beneficial tools.

I used to think I could do it all by myself. I quickly learned that I was being stubborn and egotistical. Hunting alone means you must figure everything out yourself, reinvent every wheel, and open every door through your own limited efforts. Trust me, there is no nobility in being a lone wolf. Find yourself a pack or a group of like-minded people by contacting other entrepreneurs and sales pros. Believe it or not, positive people love helping one another.

## The Power of Collaborative Hunting

In nature, wolves don't hunt alone if they're after large prey. Lions form prides to take down animals they could never conquer individually. The same principle applies in business. Collaborative hunting—networking with strategic intent—

allows you to tackle opportunities far beyond what you could approach alone.

This isn't just about knowing more people. It's about knowing the right people in the right way. When you build genuine relationships with complementary hunters, you create a force multiplier for everyone involved.

Think about it this way: If you know 100 people and each of them knows 100 people, that's potentially 10,000 connections. But the real value isn't in the number—it's in the quality and depth of those connections. One deep, trusting relationship with the right ally can be worth more than 1,000 superficial contacts.

When I decided to start selling to apartment managers, I would walk in the front door, introduce myself, and try to set up a meeting with the manager—success rate: 30% at best. After joining the local apartment association and finding like-minded sales guys from other companies, I realized the power of hunting with a pack.

This connection resulted in us facilitating a Lunch and Learn in a room full of managers. After that meeting, we sent out well over half a million dollars' worth of proposals. Had I not made these connections, I may not have had that same opportunity.

## Leveraging Professional Organizations

Building your network by joining various associations is a great tool I feel many entrepreneurs never utilize. There are many: Chamber of Commerce, Young Professionals, Rotary, and even industry-related associations are amazing resources to help you become a part of a network of other professionals, as well as something bigger than yourself.

Entrepreneurship gets lonely. Finding someone and bringing them value creates that mutualism in the market that saves you tremendously in tough times. These organizations provide structured opportunities to connect with potential mentors and allies in your industry or community.

Don't just join and attend meetings passively, though. Volunteer for committees. Speak at events. Contribute your expertise. The more value you add to the organization, the more visible you become to the established members who might become valuable connections.

When I joined my local apartment association, I didn't just attend meetings. I made sure to introduce myself to key players, volunteered for committees, and positioned myself as a valuable resource. This active approach accelerated my ability to form meaningful connections that led to business.

## Networking in the Digital Age

The digital revolution has transformed how we network, removing geographic limitations and creating new platforms for connection. Social media has become an incredible tool for finding and connecting with like-minded entrepreneurs globally.

I'm a member and regular contributor to several groups on Facebook, LinkedIn, and Discord. I've made several new friends and valuable business connections through these platforms. Here's a simple approach that works:

1. Find groups that align with your business interests or industry
2. Request to join and observe the conversations first
3. Start contributing valuable insights without immediately selling
4. Connect personally with members who share your mindset

5. Build relationships before proposing collaborations

Another huge benefit in the new era of business is having the ability to remove geographic boundaries to connect with others. You can utilize this to help grow your presence by bringing in your comrades. Video platforms like Zoom, Google Meet, or even livestreams on social media channels allow you to collaborate with people worldwide.

When you do these collaborative sessions, you experience what I call cross-pollination. Some of their audience will be new to you, likewise with your audience for them. If they like your content, they are likely to follow you and potentially become clients or partners.

This is one of the main reasons I have my podcast - it's a way for me to reach out to influential individuals and offer to put them on a pedestal while providing value to my audience. There aren't many people who don't appreciate having their expertise recognized.

## The Compound Effect of Networking

Like compound interest in finance, networking creates exponential returns over time. Each connection potentially leads to multiple new connections, each opportunity potentially leads to multiple new opportunities, and each collaboration potentially leads to deeper and more valuable collaborations.

But this compounding only works if you maintain and nurture your network consistently. Many entrepreneurs make the mistake of networking intensively when they need something, then letting their connections go cold when they don't. This approach severely limits the compound effect.

Instead, think of networking as an ongoing investment. Regular deposits of value—sharing useful information, making introductions, recognizing achievements, offering support—

ensure that your network continues to grow in both size and strength. These small, consistent actions compound over time, creating a robust ecosystem of connections that provides increasing returns.

I've experienced this firsthand. Relationships I established years ago continue to bear fruit today, often in ways I never could have anticipated when the connections were first made. A casual introduction at a conference led to a major partnership three years later. A small favor for a colleague resulted in a game-changing opportunity down the road.

## Overcoming Networking Resistance

Despite its proven benefits, many entrepreneurs resist networking. They see it as insincere, time-consuming, or outside their comfort zone. If you find yourself hesitating to network, consider reframing how you think about it.

Networking isn't about being fake or self-promotional. At its core, it's about forming genuine human connections around shared interests and goals. The most effective networkers aren't smooth-talking salespeople—they're authentic individuals who genuinely care about others and consistently provide value.

If you're naturally introverted, remember that quality matters more than quantity. You don't need to work a room of 100 people—you might be better served by having three deep conversations with the right individuals. Play to your strengths.

And if time is your concern, recognize that strategic networking should save you time in the long run by connecting you with resources, opportunities, and knowledge you'd otherwise spend much longer acquiring on your own.

## The Power of Momentum and Encouragement

Every entrepreneur will need encouragement at some point in their journey. For most, that will be at the very beginning of your journey. Our society has created a mass of people afraid to take risks. Afraid to believe in themselves. Afraid to do what others say is impossible. Your fellow friends who aren't hunters will not be much help. Many refuse to take that chance, which is either good or bad. Remember, as shared earlier, business ownership isn't meant for everyone.

Les Brown has a famous saying, "Birds of a feather flock together." This saying speaks to hunters as well. As a hunter, you will have ups and downs, and maybe one of the most important aspects of having some carnivore camaraderie is having a pack to lean on when things just aren't going well. They will be there to encourage you to keep going. Keep pushing.

Phone conversations will turn to pure gold. Bouncing ideas back and forth—letting iron sharpen iron. The ideas I will draw from hour-long discussions with my comrades have amazed me. Then, being encouraged to pursue them with the passion and drive that only hunters have.

If you can build a circle around you that increases happiness and joy while simultaneously driving out negativity and hate, you will be in an environment where fear doesn't exist. That's your biggest challenge right now—you haven't made that first or next leap because you are afraid of what might happen or what people might think. It's your life—you are in charge. Surround yourself with like-minded people, and your confidence will increase.

Mass multiplied by velocity—momentum—is the most powerful force you will ever experience in business. It's why a rock can hold a car on a hillside but stands no chance against that same car when it travels 70mph down the highway. This same principle applies to your networking. The momentum created through your association with other hunters will propel you to bigger goals and impacts—not only for yourself but for everyone you encounter.

# Why Not Everyone Can Go With You on Your Journey

Unfortunately, not everyone gets to go with you. Some family and friends will go, but not everyone. You have to reflect on the people in your life. The people from your "old ways" can't come, or you risk being weighed down. When deciding to commit 100 percent to chasing your passion, you will be on your way to being in a league of your own with the elite.

Entrepreneurship is a risky business that many people don't understand; when I decided to chase my goals as a business owner while a high school senior—friends and even a teacher—tried to talk me out of it. While there will always be naysayers, chasing and achieving your goals is up to you. It's ok to cut people off. You know who they are. Several years ago, I decided to cut loose anything and anybody holding back my growth and progress. As they say, it's lonely at the top for a hunter.

## Identifying Comrades That Need to Be Changed

Self-doubt is the kryptonite of an entrepreneur. The self-doubt will only exist in a negative environment. Unfortunately, I grew up in an environment that believed if someone was doing better than us or had more than we had or was "rich"—then they more than likely cheated, stole, or screwed someone over. This is simply being a victim on my family's part. They never stopped to look at their current situation and decided that they were a product of their choices and decisions.

Maybe instead of my cousins blowing lines and popping pills, they could have started a business. Instead of flipping weed, they could have flipped sneakers or played video games. Nevertheless, the negativity in their life was ultimately their demise. It got to a point where I had to cut them off completely. It wasn't easy, and it wasn't received well by my family, but at some point, I decided to stop playing the victim and take absolute control of my life. If it was going to be—it was up to me. You need to make the tough decision; the sooner, the better.

## The Evolution of Your Circle

I've never done a huge rebuild of my circle because it's always an ongoing progressive move as you reach new levels of success. As you set new goals for yourself, some people in your circle will naturally fall off because they aren't growing as fast as you are. That's OK, and you can't make yourself feel bad about it. We only have a finite number of years on this planet. We can't dillydally around, worrying about hurting people's feelings or what others may think of us. Be unapologetically yourself and never apologize for having big goals.

Not everyone is meant to travel at the same speed or on the same road. Creating distance from someone doesn't mean declaring them "wrong" or "bad"—it simply acknowledges that your paths are different. They may be perfect traveling companions for someone else, just not for you at this stage of your journey.

Making these decisions isn't easy, but it's necessary. The emotional challenge of creating distance from people you care about shouldn't be understated. The guilt can be overwhelming. The second-guessing can be constant. The social pressure to maintain unhealthy relationships "because that's what we do" can be enormous.

But remember this: genuine love supports growth, even when that growth creates distance. True friends want your success, even if they can't directly contribute to it. Real family celebrates your rise, even if they don't understand every step of your journey.

You have permission. Permission to outgrow relationships that no longer serve you. Permission to distance yourself from people who drain rather than energize you. Permission to choose your future over your past.

Choose wisely those who walk beside you on this hunt. Your success depends on it.

# CHAPTER 7

# The Wild Fights Back: Overcoming External and Internal Challenges

*In ages long past, when hunters ventured into untamed wilderness, they carried two weapons: the spear in their hand and the resolve in their heart. For lo, it was written that the hunter faces not one battle but two—the hunt in the wild and the hunt within. The wilderness does not discriminate between the worthy and unworthy. It presents its challenges to all who dare enter its domain. Storms rage without concern for the hunter's plans. Prey adapts without regard for the hunter's hunger. Seasons change without mercy for the hunter's preparation. Yet greater still is the wilderness within—the terrain of doubt, fear, and hesitation that must be conquered before the external hunt can succeed. The ancient scrolls speak of hunters who faltered not because their prey was too swift, but because their resolve was too weak; not because the competition was too fierce, but because their adaptation was too slow. Behold the truth etched in stone since the dawn of the hunt: The most dangerous predator is not the one that stands before you, but the one that lives inside you. The greatest competition is not with those who hunt beside you, but with who you were yesterday. The novice hunter seeks only the kill. The master hunter embraces the entire journey, finding wisdom in waiting, strength in pursuit, patience in tracking, and joy in the ultimate conquest. For what is the value of a successful hunt if the hunter returns spiritually diminished? The legendary hunters of old understood that external challenges sharpen the body, while internal challenges sharpen the soul. They faced both with equal courage, knowing that mastery of the wilderness begins with mastery of the wilderness within.*

As you venture forth into your own hunting grounds, where market forces clash like thundering herds and business challenges stalk like hidden predators, ask yourself: Do you carry both weapons? Have you prepared for both hunts? Are you ready to overcome not just what stands in your path, but also what stands in your mind?

The hunt awaits.

# Market Competition: How to Stay Ahead of the Market

## Swimming in a Sea of Competitors

There will always be competition. That's the name of the game. You might think you're going into a business or market with no one else, but you'd be foolish to think that. At Carroll Media, when we were developing Alli's AI lead detection technology, I thought we were ahead of the game. By the time we launched, there were three other companies already in the market space.

Anytime you have a first-mover advantage, you need to run fast as hell because the time is ticking. The window of opportunity doesn't stay open forever, and competitors are always watching for successful ideas they can replicate or improve upon.

Now, I still think our AI lead detection is the best on the market—it identifies names, phone numbers, email addresses, and home addresses of website visitors. But some of the market has already been gobbled up by the competition, and a certain percentage of those businesses will never change providers. First-mover advantage isn't just about being first; it's about capitalizing on that position before others can catch up.

If you're interested in checking out Alli's AI lead detection, send an email to support@carroll.media and let them know you're reading *The Hunter Head Game* and are interested in getting a free demo and trial of Alli.

Understanding your competition isn't about obsession—it's about awareness. Like a hunter who knows all the other predators in his territory, you need to understand who else is hunting in your market. Here's how I approach competitive analysis:

- **Identify who's competing for your prey.** Not everyone in your industry is your direct competition. Focus on those targeting the same customers with similar solutions.

- **Study their hunting patterns.** What marketing approaches do they use? How do they price their services? What unique value do they offer?

- **Find the gaps they've missed.** Every competitor has blind spots—opportunities they've overlooked or customer needs they're not serving well.

- **Don't fixate on the cheapest competitors.** There will always be someone willing to charge less. That's not a battle worth fighting.

The cheapest company in your market is often doing the most damage—to themselves. They're setting themselves up for long-term failure by training customers to value price over quality, establishing unsustainable margins, and likely delivering subpar service due to their cost constraints.

When I started in the power washing business, I saw competitors constantly undercutting each other's prices. Rather than join this race to the bottom, I focused on quality, reliability, and exceptional service. Yes, we lost some price-sensitive clients, but we gained loyal customers who valued results over the lowest bid.

## Finding Your Unique Advantage

The greatest hunters don't compete directly with the pack. They find their own territory, develop unique skills, or hunt in ways others haven't mastered. Your business should do the same.

Your unique advantage—what I call your "hunter's edge"—comes from understanding what makes you different and leveraging that difference. This isn't just about being better; it's about being different in ways that matter to your clients.

For me, building EasyPro (which I still own today) represented a pivot that created a unique advantage. I realized that yard care and landscaping were becoming commoditized, with low margins and intense competition. By rebranding from "Yard Smart Lawn Care and Landscaping" to "EasyPro" with the tagline "Make life easy, call a pro," I was able to differentiate my business and expand beyond our initial services.

This pivot allowed me to shift from the low-margin "green division" (lawn care and landscaping) to the highly profitable "clean division" (power washing and window cleaning). We still offer these services today to some of the largest property management companies across the Midwest and Southeast.

Your unique advantage might come from:

- Specialized expertise that others don't possess
- Superior systems that deliver more consistent results
- A unique combination of services that solve related problems
- Better client experience that creates emotional loyalty
- A distinctive approach to solving common problems

Once you identify your unique advantage, you need to become known for it. Becoming the expert in your clients' eyes isn't about claiming expertise—it's about demonstrating it consistently through your actions, content, solutions, and results.

## Winning Client Loyalty In A Competitive Landscape

Client loyalty isn't what it used to be. With more options than ever and easy access to information, today's clients can and will switch providers if they see a better alternative. The days of lifetime clients are largely over, replaced by the need to continuously earn and re-earn loyalty.

Knowing this, we've built several strategies at Carroll Media to maintain strong client relationships despite fierce competition:

- Add value beyond the transaction. We regularly share industry insights, market updates, and helpful tips with clients—even when there's nothing in it for us immediately.

- Build relationships at multiple levels. If your relationship is with just one person at a client's company, you're vulnerable if they leave. Develop connections throughout the organization.

- Address issues proactively. When something goes wrong (and eventually, something will), own it immediately and present a solution before the client has to ask.

- Consistently exceed expectations. Under promise and overdeliver—not by setting low bars, but by setting reasonable expectations and then surprising them with extraordinary service.

One of the most overlooked opportunities in competitive markets is the chance to expand business with existing clients. Many entrepreneurs focus so heavily on new client acquisition that they neglect the goldmine already in their client base.

Your clients aren't interested in up-sells or cross-sells until you tell them about it. They're focused on their own challenges, not on discovering all the ways you might help them. It's your responsibility to educate them about additional solutions you offer that might benefit them.

At EasyPro, we built a system for introducing existing landscaping clients to our power washing services at precisely the right time—typically when their property could visibly benefit from the service. This approach felt helpful rather than pushy because the need was evident, and the timing was right.

## Controlling the Hunt

In nature, hunters who control their environment succeed more often than those who simply react to circumstances. The same principle applies in business. You need to control your sales process, client interactions, and market positioning.

Too many entrepreneurs allow prospects to control the sales process, resulting in endless delays, price negotiations, and ultimately lost deals. Instead, you need to lead the hunt through what I call detection and conclusion agendas.

A discovery agenda helps you uncover the prospect's true needs, pain points, decision-making process, and buying criteria. Without this information, you're hunting blindfolded. Questions like "What's caused you to explore this service now?" and "How will you measure success if we work together?" give you the intelligence needed to position your solution effectively.

A conclusion agenda establishes clear next steps and timelines, preventing deals from stalling in indecision. This might include statements like, "Based on what we've discussed, I'll prepare a solution by Thursday. If it meets your needs, when could you make a decision?" This approach respectfully moves the process forward while giving you visibility into the real timeline.

The most common barriers that prevent prospects from buying I sum up into an acronym I learned from my first sales coach - F.U.D.:

- **Fear** of making the wrong decision

- **Uncertainty** that you're the best option available

- **Doubt** about the promised results

Your job is to systematically remove these barriers through education, proof, clarity, and differentiation. This isn't manipulation—it's helping prospects overcome the psychological obstacles that prevent them from solving their problems.

When clients see you as the best deal, it rarely means they think you're the cheapest option. Rather, they perceive that the value you deliver exceeds your price by the greatest margin compared to alternatives. This "value gap" is what makes clients choose you over competitors, even when your price is higher.

## Keeping the Pipeline Flowing

One of the most dangerous positions for a hunter is dependency on a single water source—if it dries up, survival is threatened. Similarly, entrepreneurs who depend too heavily on a few large clients or prospects put their business at risk.

Never fall in love with the food. I've seen too many entrepreneurs become fixated on landing a particular "dream client," only to neglect their broader business development efforts. While that dream deal stalls, their pipeline dries up, creating feast-or-famine cycles that destabilize the business.

The solution is to maintain a consistently flowing pipeline of opportunities at various stages. This requires:

- Systematic prospecting activities that happen regardless of how busy you are with current clients

- Regular relationship nurturing with past and present clients for referrals and repeat business

- Multiple lead generation channels so you're not dependent on a single source

- Tracking and measuring each stage of your pipeline to identify and address bottlenecks

Your closing rate—the percentage of qualified opportunities that become clients—is a critical metric to track. Industry standards vary, but in most B2B services, expect a closing rate between 20-30% for new prospects and 60-70% for existing clients.

If your closing rate falls below these levels, examine your qualification process (you may be pursuing poor-fit prospects), your value proposition (it may not be compelling enough), or your sales approach (you may be making common mistakes that kill deals).

Referrals remain the highest-quality lead source for most businesses. To generate them consistently, create a referral system rather than making occasional, awkward requests. Your best clients are usually happy to refer you—they just need to be reminded and guided through a simple process.

At Carroll Media, we've built a "Success Partnership" program where we highlight client results and then naturally transition to asking, "Who else do you know who might benefit from similar results?" This approach feels collaborative rather than transactional because it starts with celebrating their success.

In a competitive market, remember this: You don't need to outrun the bear; you just need to outrun the other hunters. By staying sharper, moving faster, adapting more quickly, and maintaining a consistently full pipeline, you'll stay ahead regardless of how crowded your hunting ground becomes.

## The Hunter's Competitive Checklist

Before you venture into your next competitive situation, review this hunter's checklist to ensure you're fully prepared:

1. **Know Your Territory:** Have you thoroughly mapped your market landscape, including all major competitors and their positions?

2. **Sharpen Your Spear:** Is your unique advantage clearly defined and consistently demonstrated to prospects?

3. **Track Your Prey:** Are you systematically gathering intelligence about prospect needs and decision processes?

4. **Scout Multiple Paths:** Have you established diverse lead sources to prevent dependency on a single channel?

5. **Mark Your Territory:** Does your brand clearly communicate your unique position in the market?

6. **Strengthen Your Pack:** Are you continuously developing your team's capabilities to deliver superior

value?

7. **Protect Your Hunting Ground:** Do you have strategies in place to retain and expand relationships with existing clients?

8. **Plan For Changing Seasons:** Have you anticipated how market conditions might shift and prepared accordingly?

The hunter who completes this checklist before each hunt significantly increases their odds of success in even the most competitive markets.

# Business Struggles: When to Pivot and When to Push Forward

### Time vs. Money: The Entrepreneur's Dilemma

As entrepreneurs, we face a fundamental truth that most people never fully grasp—time and money are interchangeable, but they're not equally valuable. You can always make more money, but you can never make more time.

I can't speak highly enough about Dan Martell's book "Buy Back Your Time." The strategies he teaches are invaluable for any entrepreneur seeking to break free from the time-for-money trap. While I may be partial because I'm in Dan's coaching company, SaaS Academy, the principles he outlines have transformed how I approach business.

In the early days of my entrepreneurial journey, I made the classic mistake of trying to do everything myself. I thought I was saving money, but I was spending something far more precious—my time. I was the guy answering phones, sending invoices, operating equipment, and meeting with clients. My business owned me rather than me owning my business.

Today, I focus on spending my profits or "money" not on things but on people and services that buy back my time. This philosophical shift has been transformative. Instead of asking, "How much does this cost?" I now ask, "How much time will this save me, and what's the value of that time?"

When evaluating whether to delegate a task or continue handling it yourself, consider these factors:

- **Dollar value of your time**: What could you earn in an hour focused on your highest-value activities?

- **Growth impact**: Could this time be spent on activities that directly grow your business?

- **Energy drain**: Does this task deplete energy you need for more important work?

- **Skill alignment**: Is this something someone else could do as well as or better than you?

The math is often surprisingly clear. If your time is worth $200/hour in revenue-generating activities, and you can hire someone at $25/hour to handle administrative tasks, every hour you spend on those tasks costs you $175 in opportunity cost. That's not savings—it's an expensive indulgence.

## Delegation as a Strategic Weapon

Delegation isn't just about offloading tasks you don't like—it's a strategic weapon that multiplies your impact and accelerates your growth. When deployed effectively, delegation allows you to focus exclusively on the activities only you can do: setting vision, building key relationships, making high-level decisions, and innovating.

The biggest obstacle to effective delegation isn't finding people—it's your own reluctance to let go. Many entrepreneurs fall into the trap of thinking, "By the time I explain how to do it, I could have just done it myself." This short-term thinking keeps them perpetually stuck in operational details.

The solution is to view delegation as an investment. Yes, it takes longer the first few times you delegate a task. You'll need to create systems, document processes, train people, and review their work. But after that initial investment, you receive compounding returns as that task is handled indefinitely without your involvement.

At Carroll Media, we've built comprehensive systems for handling post-sales paperwork—one of the most time-consuming yet necessary aspects of our business. What once consumed hours of my week is now handled by team members following documented processes. The initial time investment to create these systems was significant, but the long-term time savings have been enormous.

Effective delegation requires:

- **Clear expectations**: Define precisely what success looks like

- **Proper training**: Ensure people have the skills and knowledge they need

- **Documented processes**: Create step-by-step instructions for repeatable tasks

- **Appropriate authority**: Give people the power to make necessary decisions

- **Regular check-ins**: Provide feedback and support without micromanaging

Remember, the goal isn't just to hand off tasks—it's to build systems that continue functioning with minimal input from you. When you can take a two-week vacation and return to a business that ran smoothly in your absence, you've achieved effective delegation.

## Recognizing When to Pivot

One of the most difficult decisions any entrepreneur faces is knowing when to persist with their current approach and when to pivot. Push forward too long on a failing strategy, and you'll exhaust your resources. Pivot too quickly or too often, and you'll never gain traction.

Earlier in the book, I told you about Yard Smart Lawn Care and Landscaping, which was the business I started right out of high school. About three years into that business, I realized that I needed to provide more services than just landscaping and lawn care, but my name had pigeonholed me into that service sector.

I decided to make a pivot. I think it's OK to make pivots, and I understand that sometimes what works for you years ago isn't working anymore. The last four digits of my cell phone number at the time were 3279, which spells out "EASY." I started brainstorming ideas of company names that had "easy" in them.

This was way before the days of AI, which could've given me hundreds of ideas in a split second. But after a few long nights, I came up with "EasyPro," and the tagline would be "Make life easy, call a pro." Because at the end of the day, that's what I provided to my clients—an easy solution for their exterior services needs.

I still own EasyPro to this day. I was fortunate enough to grow the lawn care and landscaping division to over $3 million in revenue. I found a franchise buyer that bought my accounts and equipment but allowed me to retain the brand that I had built—which, between me and you, I thought had the most value out of anything in the business.

After selling off what I called the "Green Division," I focused solely on the "Clean Division" which was power washing and window cleaning. We still offer those services today to some of the largest property management companies across the Midwest and Southeast. That pivot so long ago allowed me to move out of the low-margin service and expand into a highly profitable service.

The key indicators that may signal it's time to pivot include:

- **Diminishing returns**: When increasing effort yields decreasing results

- **Market saturation**: When competition intensifies and differentiation becomes harder

- **Margin compression**: When profitability declines despite stable or growing revenue

- **Customer feedback**: When clients consistently request services you don't offer

- **Technological shifts:** When new technologies threaten to make your approach obsolete

Regularly reviewing your "Before the Hunt" plan—the vision and strategy you initially established—is essential. This isn't about abandoning your core mission but about honestly assessing whether your current approach is still the most effective path to achieving it.

A pivot doesn't necessarily mean radical reinvention. It might involve shifting to an adjacent market, expanding your service offerings, changing your delivery model, or redefining your ideal client profile. The goal is to preserve what's working while adapting what isn't.

At the end of every year at Carroll Media, we conduct a company-wide SWOT analysis to examine the Strengths, Weaknesses, Opportunities, and Threats both in the business and with each team member. Every individual on the team also does a personal SWOT analysis. This systematic approach gives us a structured way to evaluate where we stand and identify whether pivots need to occur, either at a company level or within specific aspects of our operation.

This annual ritual forces us to step back from day-to-day operations and take a comprehensive inventory of our current position. Often, opportunities for pivots emerge naturally from this process—we see gaps in the market, internal strengths we haven't fully leveraged, or emerging threats that require proactive responses.

When EasyPro pivoted from primarily lawn care to include power washing, we maintained our core promise of solving exterior maintenance problems. What changed was how we solved those problems and which specific problems we focused on solving.

## When to Double Down and Push Forward

Just as important as knowing when to pivot is recognizing when to double down on your current strategy—when to push through challenges rather than change direction. Some of the greatest business successes came after periods of significant difficulty that might have prompted less determined entrepreneurs to pivot prematurely.

Persistence is particularly important when:

- **You have evidence your approach works**: If your service clearly delivers value but faces temporary obstacles

- **The core problem you're solving remains significant**: If market need persists despite changing conditions

- **Early adoption is promising**: If initial clients show strong satisfaction and retention

- **Your solution is ahead of market readiness**: If you're innovating in ways the market hasn't fully embraced yet

Long decision processes are one of the most common challenges that test an entrepreneur's resolve. When potential clients take months to make decisions, it's easy to become discouraged and start questioning your offering.

In commercial services, I've experienced sales cycles that stretched to 18 months or longer. The key to maintaining momentum during these extended processes is to:

- **Create a mutual action plan**: Establish clear steps and timelines with the prospect's buy-in

- **Maintain regular contact**: Provide value in every interaction to stay top-of-mind

- **Engage multiple stakeholders**: Build relationships throughout the organization

- **Track and acknowledge progress:** Celebrate movement through the decision process

- **Understand the client's decision-making factors:** Know what truly drives their evaluation

Sometimes pushing forward means enduring significant discomfort. During the early days of Carroll Media, we faced several months where cash flow was tight, key deals were delayed, and market conditions were challenging. It would have been easy to retreat to something safer or pivot to a less ambitious model.

Instead, we doubled down on our core strategy, trimmed unnecessary expenses, focused intensely on client delivery, and trusted in the foundation we'd built. That period of persistence eventually gave way to accelerated growth that would not have been possible had we changed course.

## Managing Sales Quotas and Targets

The dreaded sales quota—few phrases create more anxiety for entrepreneurs and sales professionals. Yet quotas and targets serve an essential purpose: they provide clear metrics for success and create healthy pressure to perform.

The problem isn't quotas themselves, but how they're established and managed. Arbitrary quotas disconnected from market realities or business capabilities create unnecessary stress without improving results.

Instead, develop quotas based on:

- **Historical performance:** What has your business or team achieved in the past?

- **Market conditions**: What's happening in your industry and the broader economy?

- **Available resources**: What can you reasonably achieve with your current capabilities?

- **Strategic objectives**: What targets align with your long-term vision?

When I managed sales teams, I found that the most effective approach was collaborative quota-setting. Rather than imposing targets from above, I worked with each team member to establish goals they felt ownership of and commitment to.

This doesn't mean allowing people to set easy targets. It means engaging them in the process of establishing meaningful, challenging goals they believe are achievable with focused effort.

Once quotas are established, the key to achieving them is systematic activity management. Break down the final target into weekly and daily activities:

- If your quarterly revenue target is $300,000...
- And your average deal size is $15,000...
- And your closing rate is 25%...
- Then you need 80 qualified opportunities in your pipeline...
- Which might require 240 discovery calls...
- Which could mean 15 calls per day

This approach transforms an intimidating quarterly target into manageable daily activities. The focus shifts from the pressure of the end goal to the discipline of daily execution.

When you're balancing short-term targets with long-term vision, remember that quotas are a means to an end, not the end itself. They're tools to drive activity and measure progress toward your larger vision. When quotas become the sole focus, they can undermine long-term success by encouraging short-sighted decisions.

The most successful hunters don't measure their success solely by today's kill. They measure it by the health of their hunting grounds, the strength of their skills, and their ability to hunt successfully season after season. Bring this same long-term perspective to your business activities, and you'll make decisions that support sustainable growth rather than temporary target achievement.

## The Pivot Framework: Four Critical Questions

When faced with the pivotal decision of whether to persist or change direction, use this framework to clarify your thinking. Ask yourself these four critical questions:

1. **Core Mission Alignment:** Does our current approach still serve our fundamental mission, or has it become a distraction? *Consider whether you're still addressing the core problem you set out to solve, even if the method has changed.*

2. **Market Response Reality:** What is the market telling us through its behavior (not just words)? *Look at metrics like conversion rates, customer retention, and referrals—not just what prospects say they want.*

3. **Resource Sustainability:** Can we continue our current approach long enough to achieve breakthrough, or will we exhaust critical resources first? *Assess your runway, team energy, and financial reserves honestly.*

4. **Opportunity Cost:** What other opportunities are we foregoing by persisting with this approach? *Evaluate what else you could be doing with the same resources and whether that might yield better returns.*

The EasyPro pivot from "Green Division" to "Clean Division" succeeded because it maintained alignment with our core mission (exterior property services) while responding to market realities (higher margins in power washing), preserved our brand equity, and capitalized on customer relationships we'd already established.

When these four questions point toward pivot, move decisively. When they suggest persistence, double down with renewed conviction. The clarity that comes from this structured evaluation will give you confidence regardless of which path you choose.

# The Role of Adaptability In Entrepreneurial Success

## Staying Sharp in a Changing Landscape

In the wild, predators that fail to adapt to changing environments eventually starve. The same principle applies in business. Markets evolve, customer preferences shift, technologies transform, and competitors innovate. The entrepreneur who can't adapt to these changes becomes obsolete.

Staying sharp isn't optional—it's survival. This means continuously honing your skills, expanding your knowledge, and refining your approach. The moment you believe you've mastered your craft is precisely when you become vulnerable to disruption.

I've watched numerous entrepreneurs fail not because they lacked talent or work ethic, but because they refused to adapt. They became attached to their way of doing business—their hunting techniques—even as the landscape around them transformed.

The adaptability mindset begins with humility. No matter how successful you've been, recognize that yesterday's formula for success won't necessarily work tomorrow. The most adaptable hunters approach each day with beginner's eyes, looking for changes in the environment that might require a new approach.

This doesn't mean abandoning your principles or core values. In fact, clear principles enhance adaptability by providing a stable foundation from which to evolve your methods. At Carroll Media, our commitment to delivering measurable results for clients has remained constant, but how we achieve those results has evolved dramatically as technologies and market conditions have changed.

Developing mental flexibility requires deliberate practice. Here are some strategies I've found effective:

- <u>Expose yourself to diverse perspectives.</u> Read beyond your industry. Connect with people outside your usual circles. These cross-pollinations often spark innovative adaptations.

- <u>Question your assumptions regularly</u>. Ask, "What if the opposite were true?" This mental exercise helps loosen rigid thinking patterns.

- <u>Run small experiments frequently</u>. Test new approaches at low risk before committing significant resources.

- <u>Study adaptable companies outside your industry.</u> What allowed them to evolve successfully while competitors failed?

- <u>Develop scenario planning skills.</u> Regularly imagine different possible futures and how you might respond to each.

The rigid hunter starves not because of a lack of prey, but because of an inability to hunt differently. Don't let your past success formula become tomorrow's failure recipe.

## Adapting to Client Behaviors

One of the most crucial areas requiring adaptability is in how you respond to changing client behaviors. These shifts occur constantly, sometimes gradually and sometimes suddenly, requiring corresponding shifts in your approach.

Consider how client communication preferences have evolved. Just a decade ago, phone calls and emails were the primary channels. Today, clients might prefer texts, video calls, social media DMs, Slack channels, or any number of platforms. The adaptable entrepreneur meets clients where they are rather than insisting they communicate on the entrepreneur's preferred terms.

Unresponsive clients present a particular challenge that tests your adaptability. When prospects or clients stop returning calls or emails, many entrepreneurs fall into rigid response patterns: they either continue the same outreach approach (hoping for different results) or they give up entirely.

The adaptive approach is to vary your outreach method, timing, and message. If emails aren't working, try a text. If morning outreach gets no response, try late afternoon. If business-focused messages are ignored, perhaps a more personal connection might break through. Each non-response is data that should inform your next attempt.

Budget constraints ("not in the budget") represent another client behavior that demands adaptability. When I first encountered this objection early in my career, I had one basic response: offer a modest discount. This one-dimensional approach limited my effectiveness.

Today, we have multiple adaptive responses to budget concerns:

- **Timeline adjustment**: "Could we adjust the timeline to align with your next budget cycle?"

- **Scope modification**: "What version of this solution would fit your current budget constraints?"

- **Performance-based pricing**: "What if we tied our compensation to the results we deliver?"

- **Budget reallocation**: "Are there other initiatives that might be lower priority than this one?"

- **Multi-phase approach**: "Could we start with a smaller phase that fits the current budget?"

Each client and situation requires a different adaptive response. The hunter who has only one approach to tracking prey will go hungry when conditions change.

## Sales System Adaptability

While having sales systems is crucial for scalability and consistency, those systems must themselves be adaptable. Rigid sales processes that can't flex to accommodate different situations become liabilities rather than assets.

The solution is to build your sales systems with adaptability engineered into them. At Carroll Media, we've developed a core sales methodology that includes deliberate decision points where the approach can be customized based on specific client characteristics, market conditions, and competitive factors.

This looks like a decision tree rather than a linear process. At each key junction, our team evaluates the situation and selects the most appropriate path forward. The system provides structure and consistency while allowing for situational adaptation.

Negotiation tactics particularly benefit from this adaptable approach. Different client types respond to different negotiation styles:

- Analytical clients value data-driven discussions and detailed ROI analysis

- Relational clients respond to stories, social proof, and connection-based approaches

- Driver clients want bottom-line impact and direct communication

- Expressive clients appreciate vision, innovation, and creative solutions

The keys to successful negotiation lie in this adaptive flexibility—understanding when to use which approach and how to switch approaches when the current one isn't working.

In my experience, the most effective negotiators aren't those with the most aggressive tactics or strongest positions—they're those who can read the room and adapt their approach in real-time as negotiations unfold.

Chris Voss, former FBI hostage negotiator and author of "Never Split the Difference," exemplifies this adaptive negotiation approach. He teaches tactical empathy—the ability to understand the other party's position and adapt your approach accordingly. This doesn't mean compromising your objectives; it means finding the most effective path to achieving them based on the specific situation.

## Technological and Market Adaptation

Technology changes at a pace that can overwhelm entrepreneurs, especially those who aren't naturally tech-oriented. Yet technological adaptation is non-negotiable in today's business environment.

The challenge is distinguishing between technologies that represent fundamental shifts requiring adaptation and those that are merely distractions. Not every new platform, tool, or trend deserves your attention or resources.

At Carroll Media, we evaluate new technologies through these lenses:

- **Client impact**: How will this improve our ability to deliver value?

- **Efficiency gain**: Will this significantly reduce time or cost to serve clients?

- **Competitive advantage**: Does this create meaningful differentiation?

- **Strategic alignment**: Does this advance our long-term vision?

- **Implementation feasibility**: Can we reasonably integrate this into our operations?

This framework helps us be early adopters of truly important technologies while avoiding the "shiny object syndrome" that distracts many entrepreneurs.

When we developed our AI lead detection technology, we weren't first to market. But we recognized the fundamental shift this technology represented in how businesses could identify and connect with prospects. We adapted by developing our own superior version rather than ignoring the change.

Viewing your business through the windshield rather than the rearview mirror is essential for technological and market adaptation. Too many entrepreneurs make decisions based primarily on historical data rather than forward-looking indicators.

The windshield perspective involves:

- Monitoring leading indicators that predict future conditions

- Tracking emerging technologies before they become mainstream

- Studying adjacent industries for trends that might cross over

- Learning from early adopter clients whose needs often foreshadow broader market shifts

- Engaging with thought leaders who are shaping future directions

This forward-looking approach allows you to adapt proactively rather than reactively—positioning your business ahead of changes rather than scrambling to catch up after they've occurred.

## Adapting Your Resource Allocation

Perhaps the most crucial adaptation involves how you allocate your limited resources—time, money, energy, and attention—as your business evolves. The resource allocation that worked in the startup phase will cripple your growth phase. The investments that drove your growth phase may undermine your maturity phase.

The key is to regularly reassess your resource allocation based on your current stage and objectives rather than continuing historical patterns by default.

When I started EasyPro, I allocated about 70% of my time to direct service delivery, 20% to sales, and 10% to administration. As we grew, continuing this allocation would have created a ceiling on our growth. I progressively shifted to 40% sales, 40% team development, and 20% strategic planning—dramatically changing how I invested my time as our needs evolved. Now I'm 97% team development and only speak with a few key clients. But this business is in a very mature stage and has been optimized over almost two decades.

Knowing when to invest in growth versus when to focus on profitability represents another critical resource allocation adaptation. There are seasons for aggressive expansion and seasons for consolidation. The adaptable entrepreneur recognizes which season they're in and adjusts accordingly.

At Carroll Media, we are reinvesting nearly every dollar of profit into growth—hiring ahead of revenue, developing new capabilities, and expanding our market presence. We are in full blown growth mode. So, this is what is demanded.

The distinction between strategic and tactical adaptation is important here. Strategic adaptation involves fundamental shifts in your business model, market position, or value proposition. Tactical adaptation involves adjustments to how you execute your strategy.

Both are necessary, but confusing them creates problems. Don't make tactical changes when strategic adaptation is required, and don't disrupt your entire strategy when simple tactical adjustments would suffice.

When our power washing client base began requesting window cleaning services, adding this capability was a tactical adaptation that fit within our existing strategy of providing comprehensive exterior maintenance solutions. We didn't change our strategic approach to now become a window cleaning first business. Knee jerk reaction or as I call it "throwing hand grenades" in your business for no reason - is uncalled for and often becomes costly.

The most adaptable hunters know when to adjust their technique versus when to hunt different prey in new territory. This discernment comes from regular assessment of both tactical results and strategic positioning—always with an eye toward the evolving landscape rather than just the current hunt.

## The Adaptation Framework: Principles vs. Practices

The key to successful adaptation lies in understanding the crucial distinction between your principles (which should remain relatively stable) and your practices (which must continuously evolve). This framework provides clarity about what to preserve and what to change:

<u>Principles (Remain Stable):</u>

- Your core mission and purpose
- Your fundamental values and ethics
- Your key differentiators and strengths
- Your long-term vision

<u>Practices (Continuously Evolve):</u>

- Technologies and tools you employ
- Specific methods of service delivery
- Marketing and sales approaches
- Operational procedures
- Resource allocation models

At Carroll Media, our principle of "measurable client impact" has remained constant, while our practices for achieving this impact have evolved dramatically—from traditional marketing methods to AI-driven lead generation and analytics.

When you maintain clarity about this distinction, adaptation becomes less threatening. You're not abandoning who you are or what you stand for; you're simply finding more effective ways to express those core principles in a changing environment.

The hunter who understands this distinction retains their identity while continuously evolving their methods—adapting not because of weakness but because of wisdom.

# The Thrill of the Hunt: Finding Joy in the Process

True hunters understand a fundamental truth that escapes many entrepreneurs: the hunt itself is the reward, not merely the kill. When you find joy in the process—the tracking, the pursuit, the strategic positioning—you develop resilience that carries you through inevitable challenges.

Pride has no place in sales or business. This might seem counterintuitive, but the most successful hunters approach their craft with humility rather than ego. Pride blinds you to weaknesses, prevents adaptation, and creates resistance to learning. The humble hunter remains teachable, sees reality clearly, and continuously improves.

I've watched many talented entrepreneurs fail because their pride prevented them from making necessary adjustments. They became so attached to their initial vision or approach that they couldn't evolve when circumstances demanded it. They confused pride with conviction, failing to recognize that true conviction includes the courage to change methods when necessary.

In contrast, finding meaning in daily challenges transforms entrepreneurship from a series of obstacles into a journey of growth. Each problem becomes an opportunity to develop new skills, deepen your understanding, and strengthen your capabilities. This perspective shift doesn't make challenges easier, but it makes them purposeful.

The hunter's mindset involves cultivating a healthy obsession with improvement. Not perfectionism, which paralyzes, but a commitment to becoming incrementally better each day. This healthy obsession creates momentum through small daily advances rather than aiming for occasional major breakthroughs.

I practice this through my "1% Better" approach—identifying one small improvement I can make each day in my processes, client interactions, or personal capabilities. These micro-improvements compound over time, creating significant progress without the pressure of dramatic transformations.

This mindset extends beyond business results to my own character development. The hunt shapes the hunter as much as the hunter shapes the hunt. The challenges you overcome, the resilience you develop, and the wisdom you gain through experience gradually transform you into someone capable of greater achievements.

The journey matters more than the destination because the journey creates the person who ultimately arrives. The destination itself will likely evolve as you grow, but the capacity to pursue worthy objectives with skill and determination remains consistent regardless of which specific prey you're tracking.

## The Joy of the Perfect Kill

While finding joy in the process is essential, there's undeniable satisfaction in a successful "kill"—closing the deal, launching the product, solving the problem, or achieving the objective. These moments of completion provide validation, momentum, and energy for the next hunt.

Celebrating these wins is not just enjoyable; it's strategic. Each success builds confidence, reinforces effective behaviors, and creates positive emotional associations with the challenging work of entrepreneurship. The hunter who never acknowledges successful kills misses an important source of motivation.

I have developed rituals in my businesses for celebrating different types of wins:

- **New client acquisitions**: Ringing a physical bell and company-wide acknowledgment

- **Project completions**: Team lunches with specific recognition of key contributions

- **Revenue milestones**: Quarterly celebrations with rewards tied to achievement

These celebrations weren't just about making people feel good—although that mattered too. They were about reinforcing what success looked like and building a culture that recognized and replicated effective approaches.

The satisfaction of helping clients solve problems represents a particularly meaningful type of "kill" for service-based entrepreneurs. When you fundamentally improve a client's condition through your expertise and effort, the resulting satisfaction goes beyond financial rewards to a deeper sense of purpose.

I've found that this client-focused perspective creates a virtuous cycle. When you genuinely focus on solving clients' problems, most sales obstacles naturally dissolve. Resistance decreases, trust increases, and the relationship becomes collaborative rather than adversarial.

This doesn't mean you shouldn't care about your business objectives or revenue goals. It means you recognize that the most reliable path to achieving them runs through creating significant client value. The hunter who helps his tribe eat not only eats himself but gains status, influence, and long-term security.

The perfect kill in business isn't just making the sale; it's creating outcomes so valuable that clients become advocates, team members become inspired, and you yourself become more capable and confident for the next hunt.

## Maintaining Enthusiasm During Long Hunts

Entrepreneurship is not a sprint; it's a series of ultramarathons. Many business objectives require sustained effort over extended periods—sometimes years—before yielding significant results. Maintaining enthusiasm during these long hunts separates successful entrepreneurs from those who start strong but fade before reaching their objectives.

The key is finding the optimal balance between challenge and skill—what psychologists call the "flow state." When challenges slightly exceed current capabilities, you experience engagement without overwhelming stress. When challenges far exceed capabilities, anxiety results. When capabilities far exceed challenges, boredom sets in.

The ideal entrepreneurial experience involves deliberately managing this balance—continuously increasing challenges as capabilities grow. This progressive challenge approach maintains engagement while building capacity. It's why video games level up difficulty as players improve—the same principle applies to business challenges.

I apply this approach through my "progressive challenge matrix"—a framework that helps me and my team members identify our current capability level and match it with appropriately challenging work. As we master each level, the challenge increases accordingly, maintaining the optimal tension that produces growth and engagement.

Creating conditions for peak performance involves more than just challenge calibration. It also requires:

- **Clear objectives**: Knowing exactly what success looks like

- **Immediate feedback**: Seeing the results of your actions quickly

- **Undistracted focus**: Eliminating interruptions during key work

- **Skill-task alignment**: Working in areas where you have relevant capabilities

- **Autonomy**: Having control over how you approach challenges

When these conditions align, you can experience remarkable productivity and satisfaction even during difficult work. This state doesn't eliminate the effort required, but it transforms that effort from draining to energizing.

Building support systems for the long hunt is equally important for maintaining enthusiasm. No hunter can maintain peak performance indefinitely without rest, reflection, and renewal. The entrepreneur who attempts to operate at maximum intensity without appropriate recovery inevitably burns out.

My support system includes:

- **Peer group**: Fellow entrepreneurs who understand the unique challenges of this path

- **Mentors**: More experienced individuals who provide perspective and wisdom

- **Personal practices**: Regular exercise, reflection time, and complete disconnection periods

- **Family support**: Clear boundaries between work and family time, with full presence in each

- **Professional development**: Continuous learning that renews perspective and energy

These support structures don't just help you endure the long hunt—they help you thrive through it, finding joy and meaning in the journey rather than merely surviving until some distant destination.

## Learning from Master Hunters

Studying those who "kill it" in competitive markets provides invaluable insights into both the technical aspects of business success and the psychological approaches that sustain enthusiasm through challenges.

In every industry, there are entrepreneurs who consistently outperform despite facing the same external conditions as everyone else. These master hunters haven't discovered some secret hunting ground unknown to others. They've developed superior hunting techniques, mindsets, and systems that allow them to succeed where others struggle.

I've made it a practice throughout my career to study these exceptional performers—not just through books and courses, but through direct observation and relationship whenever possible. This has often required investing significant time and money, but the return on these investments has been extraordinary.

Some of the patterns I've observed among master hunters include:

- They love the game itself, not just the outcomes. Their enthusiasm comes from the challenge as much as the rewards.

- They maintain extreme ownership, never blaming external factors for results they can influence.

- They balance strategic patience with tactical urgency, knowing when to wait and when to strike.

- They operate from principles rather than tactics, adapting methods while maintaining core values.

- They continuously refine their approach based on results rather than becoming attached to techniques.

Learning from master negotiators has been particularly valuable in my development. Negotiation represents a microcosm of entrepreneurship—balancing firmness with flexibility, self-interest with relationship building, and immediate gains with long-term positioning.

Among the best negotiators I've studied, several universal principles emerge:

- Listening reveals more leverage than talking. Understanding the other party's true priorities opens paths to agreement.

- Emotional control determines outcomes. The negotiator who remains calm holds an inherent advantage.

- Creative optionality trumps brute force. Finding non-obvious solutions that satisfy both parties' core needs creates superior outcomes.

- Preparation creates confidence. The more thoroughly you understand all aspects of the negotiation context, the more comfortably you can navigate it.

- Patience is power. Rushing to agreement almost always weakens your position and results.

These negotiation principles apply far beyond formal deal-making to essentially all aspects of entrepreneurship—from client relationships to team development to strategic partnerships.

The wisdom of these master hunters reminds us that while tactics evolve with changing conditions, certain timeless principles of success remain consistent across eras. Today's digital landscape may look nothing like the business environment of previous generations, but the fundamental dynamics of value creation, relationship building, and strategic positioning remain remarkably similar.

## The Deeper Purpose of the Hunt

Ultimately, the greatest joy in entrepreneurship comes from connecting your daily activities to deeper meaning beyond transactional success. When your work becomes a vehicle for personal growth, positive impact, and legacy creation, even the most challenging aspects take on new significance.

Finding meaning beyond the transaction transforms difficult clients from frustrations into growth opportunities, market challenges from threats into purpose-defining moments, and failures from discouragement into valuable lessons. This meaning-centered perspective doesn't eliminate difficulty, but it fundamentally changes how you experience it.

The hunt can serve many deeper purposes:

- Personal development: Becoming more capable, resilient, and wise through business challenges

- Team elevation: Helping others develop their full potential through meaningful work

- Client transformation: Creating significant positive change in clients' businesses and lives

- Industry advancement: Pushing your field forward through innovation and leadership

- Community impact: Using business success to strengthen the broader community

When your hunt serves purposes beyond simply "making the kill," you discover reserves of energy, creativity, and persistence that wouldn't be available for purely transactional objectives.

The legacy of successful entrepreneurship extends far beyond financial outcomes. The businesses you build, the people you develop, the problems you solve, and the example you set create ripple effects that continue long after specific achievements fade from memory.

This legacy perspective helps maintain enthusiasm during difficult periods because you see current challenges as part of a larger narrative that transcends immediate circumstances. The day-to-day difficulties matter, but they exist within a broader context of meaning that sustains your commitment.

In my own journey, I've found that connecting business activities to legacy creation transforms how I experience entrepreneurship. Challenges become chapters in a larger story rather than isolated problems. Setbacks become plot twists rather than endpoints. The entire journey takes on narrative meaning that transcends individual hunts.

This doesn't mean becoming detached from practical realities or immediate objectives. It means viewing those practical matters through a lens that reveals their connection to deeper purpose—seeing how today's specific sales challenge or operational problem fits within your broader mission.

The journey ultimately matters more than the destination because the journey is where life happens. The destination serves primarily to give direction and meaning to the journey rather than being the point of the journey itself.

When you embrace this perspective, you discover that the greatest thrill of the hunt isn't capturing prey but becoming the kind of hunter who can pursue worthy objectives with skill, wisdom, and joy—regardless of which specific prey you're tracking at any given moment.

## Reconnecting With Your Purpose During Difficult Hunts

Even the most passionate entrepreneurs occasionally lose connection with their deeper purpose during challenging periods. When the daily grind becomes overwhelming or multiple setbacks accumulate, enthusiasm can fade and the hunt can begin to feel more like a burden than a calling.

During these inevitable difficult seasons, successful hunters have specific practices for reconnecting with their deeper purpose. These aren't just motivational tactics but practical disciplines that restore perspective and renew energy:

**1. Return to Origin Stories:** Regularly revisit why you started this journey in the first place. At Carroll Media, I keep a journal with stories of our earliest client wins and the problems we set out to solve. During challenging periods, reading these accounts reconnects me with our original purpose.

**2. Seek Direct Client Impact:** Nothing reignites purpose faster than directly experiencing the positive impact of your work. Schedule time with clients who have benefited most from your services. Hearing their stories firsthand renews the emotional connection to your deeper purpose.

**3. Advance Your Vision Through Hardship:** Frame current challenges as necessary steps toward your larger vision. I've found that writing down exactly how overcoming today's specific obstacle advances my long-term mission transforms my relationship with difficulty.

**4. Practice Gratitude for Opportunity:** The privilege of entrepreneurship – the freedom to create, lead, and build – is unavailable to many. Developing a regular gratitude practice for this opportunity shifts focus from what's difficult to what's possible.

When implementing these practices during my most challenging business periods – like the months following the 2008 financial crisis or during the early pandemic uncertainty – I discovered they don't just restore motivation temporarily. They fundamentally transform how I experience challenges, integrating them into a meaningful narrative of purposeful growth.

The hunter who maintains connection with deeper purpose doesn't just endure difficult hunts – they find unexpected meaning, growth, and even joy within them.

Essentially, the successful hunter masters both the external and internal challenges of the hunt. Externally, you learn to navigate competitive landscapes, adapt to changing conditions, and develop superior hunting techniques. Internally, you cultivate resilience, combat fear, and find joy in the process itself.

These dual mastery paths aren't separate journeys but intertwined aspects of the same pursuit. Your internal state affects how you perceive and respond to external challenges. The external challenges you face shape your internal development. Together, they form the complete education of the hunter.

The marketplace will always present obstacles—competitors who challenge your territory, conditions that change without warning, prey that grows more elusive. These external challenges aren't impediments to your success; they're the very forge that shapes you into a more capable hunter.

Similarly, the internal obstacles—doubt, fear, impatience—aren't weaknesses to be ashamed of but opportunities for developing greater self-mastery. The strongest hunters aren't those who never experience these internal challenges but those who learn to navigate them skillfully.

As you continue your entrepreneurial journey, remember that both the external and internal hunts are perpetual. There is no final state of having "arrived" where challenges cease. There is only the ongoing adventure of the hunt, with each success building capacity for the next challenge.

The true prize isn't a particular achievement or conquest, but the hunter you become through persistent engagement with worthy challenges. When you embrace both the external and internal dimensions of the hunt, entrepreneurship transforms from merely making a living into truly crafting a life—one worthy of the magnificent capabilities that lie dormant within you until challenges call them forth.

Now, return to your hunting grounds with renewed purpose. The obstacles before you are not your enemies but your teachers. The competition around you is not your adversary but your stimulus. The hunt itself is not your burden but your privilege.

Above all, remember: A hunter finds joy not despite the challenges, but because of them.

# CHAPTER 8

# From Prey to Predator: Transforming from the Hunted to the Hunter

*And the hunted cried out in the wilderness, not for rescue—but for revelation. For the beast within does not beg—it awakens.*

*Long did he wander, cloaked in fear, fleeing shadows that wore the faces of failure, doubt, and despair. He mistook motion for progress, and busyness for purpose. Yet the more he fled, the more the echo of the hunt called from within.*

*Until came the day when he could run no more. He stood not at the mercy of the world, but at the mercy of his own delay.*

*And lo, the wind whispered not warnings, but invitations. The fire did not burn to destroy, but to refine.*

*The hunted became still. And in that stillness, a decision was forged.*

*No longer would he seek shelter beneath the leaves of excuses. No longer would he bow to the tyranny of "almost" and "not yet." No longer would he wear the garments of prey.*

*He tore from himself the skins of limitation and rose not with fury—but with focus.*

*Not with rage—but with resolve.*

*The hunted life ends the moment you choose to face it.*

*The hunter's life begins when you dare to become it.*

There's a moment in every hunter's life when the old skin no longer fits. When the mask cracks. When the tools you've used to survive won't take you one step further.

Mine came wrapped in lawsuits, debt, and a business collapse that left me staring into the abyss with one brutal realization:

No one is coming to save you.

By the time I lost the gym, I had already proven I could build something. I'd taken a struggling business, tripled its members, and flipped the entire operation into a six-figure machine. But when it all came crashing down? There were no applause, no backup plan, no safety net. Just silence.

And in that silence, I met someone new. Someone more dangerous. Someone hungrier. Someone who finally understood: the most powerful thing that can happen in your life is for everything safe and familiar to burn to the ground.

Because only then do you discover who the hell you really are.

## Death Before Domination

If you want to evolve, something in you must die. That's not poetic. That's process.

Most people want growth without loss. They want transformation without the tear-down. But that's not how hunters are made.

To become a killer in business, in life, in leadership—you must be willing to bury the part of you that only wanted to be liked, to stay safe, to be fed.

The old you wanted security.

The new you chooses power.

## Burn the Blueprint

When the gym collapsed, so did my identity. I had to confront the hard truth: the blueprint I was building my life on wasn't designed to withstand real pressure.

And that's where a lot of people live—with lives, businesses, and mindsets that are one tough season away from total failure. They're still building with old tools, outdated strategies, and stories that don't serve them anymore.

Let me say this bluntly:

If your life falls apart when things get hard, then it wasn't built right.

The hunter doesn't just bounce back—he upgrades. He scraps the old map and draws a new one from the ashes.

## The Upgrade Equation

You don't need to fix the old you.

You need to replace the old you.

Here's the shift:

>   Pain + Purpose + Persistence = Power.

That's the real formula.

Pain reveals what needs to go. Purpose gives you a new direction. Persistence is the daily kill.

Put those together and you'll stop asking for a handout from life and start demanding a seat at the apex table.

## The Death Ritual

No, we're not lighting candles and chanting. But this is serious work. This is where the hunted version of you dies.

Take five minutes and write this down:

- What beliefs have been keeping you small?
- What habits no longer serve your future?
- What relationships, routines, or rules do you need to break?

That list? That's your funeral.

Now, flip the page and write your reintroduction.

- Who are you becoming?
- What will you no longer tolerate?
- What code will you live by?

This is your new operating system. You're not patching software—you're swapping the hard drive.

## Coach Carroll's Razor

Here's a little rule I live by now:

- If it doesn't align with the hunter I'm becoming, it doesn't belong in my life.

That's it. That's the filter.

It applies to decisions, to people, to opportunities, to excuses.

Try it for a week. Watch how quickly clarity comes.

After the gym, I didn't crawl back to comfort. I got meaner. Sharper. Smarter.

I pushed into EasyPro & Carroll Media with a fire in my belly that no Harvard case study could teach. Because when you've buried a dream and come back breathing, you don't fear failure anymore. You expect it. You plan for it. You leverage it.

The hunter isn't afraid of starting over. He's afraid of staying the same.

And so, I ask you:

What part of you needs to die for the next version of you to rise?

Not tomorrow.

Now.

# Strategies to Build Confidence and Competence

Confidence isn't something you wait around to feel—it's something you earn through action. Competence isn't a personality trait—it's a skillset you build brick by brick. If you want to move from the hunted to the hunter, you have to stop waiting to feel ready. You don't need permission. You need movement.

Too many people are waiting for a green light. For someone to tell them they're good enough. For some divine signal that now is the time. But here's the truth: confidence is built in the doing, not the thinking. The longer you wait, the more you validate the lie that you're not capable.

You gain confidence every time you keep your word to yourself. When you say you'll wake up early—and you do. When you say you'll make those ten sales calls—and you do. When you decide you're done tolerating mediocrity—and you act on it. That's how you start stacking wins, and those wins build your identity as someone who does what they say.

This isn't about toxic hustle or pretending you're bulletproof. It's about doing hard things with intention. Hunters don't become killers by watching YouTube videos or journaling about their goals. They do it by putting in the reps, failing fast, and recalibrating quicker.

Let's talk about skill. Competence is what breeds sustainable confidence. You don't just need to believe in yourself—you need to back it up with results. That means identifying what matters in your game and getting unreasonably good at it. Want to lead a team? Learn how to clearly communicate vision and standards. Want to close deals? Master discovery, objections, and closing. Want to scale a business? Understand cash flow, delegation, and hiring the right killers around you.

Don't spread yourself thin trying to be good at everything. Specialize. Dominate your lane. Earn your confidence through capability.

Now let's be real: confidence and competence don't come from comfort. They come from being in the arena, taking hits, and showing up again anyway. Every time you face resistance and push forward, you become a little more dangerous. A little more unshakeable.

I'm not telling you this from a mountaintop—I've lived it. When I lost the gym, I could have disappeared. But instead, I built something better. I didn't feel confident when I started over. I felt raw, exposed, and borderline broken. But I moved anyway. And that motion—those little daily wins—stacked into a confidence that couldn't be taken away.

You don't need to become someone else. You need to become who you were before the world convinced you to play small. Strip away the fear. Cut out the noise. Focus on execution. That's where your power lives.

## Dress Like the Hunter You Are

Style might seem like a small detail to some, but make no mistake—how you present yourself impacts how the world receives you and how you see yourself. As Tom Ford once said, "Dressing well is a form of good manners." It's also a form of preparation and power.

When I walk into a room, I want my presence to hit before I speak. That's why I work with Jordan Yocum, my Tom James tailor, who's not only kept me looking sharp but is also the top sales rep in the entire company. That's intentional. You want to build your tribe with the best, and Jordan is a perfect example of that. I don't just preach excellence—I surround myself with it.

Dressing well isn't about ego. It's about alignment. You want to feel like the hunter? Then look like the damn hunter. Show up with intention. Your clothes are armor. Your style is signal. Walk into every room already communicating what you stand for.

You want confidence? Do what you said you would do. You want competence? Get better on purpose.

You don't wait your way into being a hunter. You work your way into it.

And it starts today.

# The Predator Mentality: Outthinking and Outworking the Competition

The hunter does not wait. He does not wander. He does not hope. He stalks.

If you want to rise above the average, you have to think beyond the average. That means moving with intention—not just grinding for the sake of grinding, but being ruthlessly strategic about your time, your energy, and your objectives.

This is where the predator separates from the prey. It's not about being the loudest in the room. It's about being the one with the sharpest mind and the clearest plan. Strategy is what turns ambition into execution.

I didn't always get this. In fact, for years I thought outworking the competition meant doing more, sleeping less, burning both ends of the candle until there was nothing left but ash. But I learned—thankfully before it was too late—that working smarter isn't some soft excuse. It's the most lethal skillset a hunter can have.

When I joined the Endeavor ScaleUp program, our company was selected as one of just four businesses in the region. That's where I was introduced to Linda. She wasn't just any mentor—she had run Accent Marketing, a $100 million per year operation. That's the level of firepower I'm talking about when I say you need the right people in your corner.

Now, let me be clear—Linda didn't teach me EOS. We were already running our own stripped-down, re-engineered version of the Entrepreneurial Operating System before I started working with her. But what she brought to the table sharpened my thinking and helped me mature my systems.

Here's how we do it:

We don't plan blindly. We start each quarter by mapping out all the time off—team vacations, major holidays, big events, and travel plans. That gives us a realistic understanding of the runway we're working with.

Then we throw every big idea up on a whiteboard. No filters. Just raw ambition.

From there, the debate begins. The team challenges the ideas. We push, pull, and punch holes in every objective until what's left are the priorities that can move the needle. Once the dust settles, those become our quarterly rocks.

Then we work backwards.

We carve those rocks into monthly targets, and then break those into weekly commitments. Everyone knows what they're chasing, how it ladders up, and what success looks like in tangible terms. That's how we stay sharp. That's how we keep our edge.

Let me tell you something that's going to upset the get-rich-quick crowd on TikTok: there's no shortcut. There's no hack. There's no passive path to dominance. I'm not blowing smoke up your ass—I'm lighting a fire under it.

You want to build something real? It's going to take work. You want to scale a business that lasts? You'll need more than motivation—you'll need strategy, structure, and relentless execution.

That kind of strategic hunger goes all the way back to the garden.

## Even in Eden, There Was Work

Let's bring God into the boardroom for a moment.

Genesis 2:15 (NIV) says: *"The Lord God took the man and put him in the Garden of Eden to work it and take care of it."*

Even in paradise—before sin, before struggle, before scarcity—there was still work. Think about that. God didn't hand Adam a recliner and a remote. He gave him a job. A responsibility. A role in creation.

Work is not a punishment. It's a divine pattern. A calling. And when you work with purpose, when you hunt with intention, you tap into something holy.

When people tell you that business is just a grind, or that success is about luck, you can remind them that even the first man in the first garden had to put his hands to the earth. And so do you.

Strategic thinking is your spiritual inheritance. Execution is your act of worship.

That's the predator mentality. Not just hungry. Not just relentless. But calculated.

If you want to outlast and outmaneuver everyone else in your space, you can't just chase every rabbit that runs by. You have to know which one is worth the arrow.

The hunted react. The hunter plans.

So, what's your next move?

# CHAPTER 9

# Life as a Hunter: The Entrepreneurial Lifestyle

*And lo, the hunter came upon a world not of wilderness and beast, but of blinking screens and shadowed corridors.*

*Where once the hunt was for food, now it was for freedom.*

*Where once the village was guarded by spear and flame, now it is guarded by passwords and policies—yet no less dangerous, and far more deceptive.*

*The old path has grown cold. The herd follows glowing signs and silent orders. They shuffle from desk to dinner, from paycheck to pacifier, whispering of dreams they dare not pursue. They eat, but do not feast. They move, but do not hunt.*

*But you—child of fire, child of motion—you were not born for the pasture.*

*You were not born to ask permission for your breath.*

*You were not built to survive.*

*You were shaped to stalk, to rise, to claim.*

*In this new land, the terrain is unfamiliar, but the law is the same: those who hesitate are devoured. Those who act—who adapt—who awaken with the discipline of the old world and the weapons of the new—they do not merely survive...*

*They dominate.*

*For the hunt is not what you do. It is what you are.*

And so, begins the next chapter of the hunt.

There comes a moment when the hunt is more than a tactic—it becomes a way of life.

In the new era of business, entrepreneurship isn't just a career path. It's a full-contact identity shift. It demands more than a polished elevator pitch and a LinkedIn headline. It demands your whole being—your energy, your habits, your relationships, and most of all, your perspective.

This chapter is about that shift. It's about building a life designed for domination, not just participation. It's about becoming the kind of person whose very existence demands attention, respect, and results.

## Understanding the New Era of Business

The rules have changed.

There have been three technological tidal waves that reshaped the battlefield.

### The First Wave: The Internet

This was the dawn of the digital age. The Internet broke the gates wide open—eliminating traditional gatekeepers and giving everyone with a connection a chance to compete. Thank you sacred AOL free trial CD.

You didn't need a storefront to sell. You didn't need permission to publish. It democratized access. With nothing but a laptop and a Wi-Fi signal, anyone could build something real. Google became the classroom. Email replaced door-knocking. Websites became 24/7 salespeople.

This wave wasn't just about efficiency—it was about empowerment. A teenager in their bedroom suddenly had the same reach as a Fortune 500 brand. For the modern hunter, it was the first spear.

## The Second Wave: Social Media

Next came attention. And in the attention economy, he who captures the scroll wins the gold.

Platforms like Facebook, Instagram, YouTube, and now TikTok turned everyday people into global broadcasters. Personality became profit. Visibility became currency. For the first time ever, brand was built in real-time. Not in boardrooms, but in bedrooms. Not with billboards, but with iPhones.

I've been screaming this since 2013—social media is the single greatest gift to the modern small business owner. The algorithm doesn't care if you've got a trust fund or a Shopify trial. If your message hits, it spreads. It's David with a digital slingshot.

## The Third Wave: Artificial Intelligence

And now? Now comes the reckoning.

AI isn't a trend—it's a paradigm shift. And I'm not preaching this from some ivory tower. I'm writing this very book with help from ChatGPT. Some might say that's cheating. I say it's sharpening my spear.

Tools like OpenAI, Anthropic, and Perplexity are reinventing how we think, sell, build, market, and serve. If you're not adapting, you're already losing. Period.

To ignore AI today would be like refusing to use electricity in the 1900s. That's not bold—that's suicidal. Don't be the plumber in 2008 who didn't think he needed a website. Don't be the realtor in 2013 who ignored Facebook Ads. Don't be the business owner in 2025 who says, "AI just isn't for me."

***Access. Attention. AI.*** These are the arenas now. This is the battlefield. Choose your weapons wisely.

## Breaking Free from the 9-to-5 Mindset

Let's get one thing straight: this isn't a knock on the 9-to-5. There are honorable people working hard jobs with honest pay. But if you're reading this book, you're not wired for clocking in and clocking out.

You were built to hunt.

But even when people leave the corporate world, they often carry the mindset with them. They look for permission. They wait for instructions. They expect predictable outcomes from minimal effort.

That's not how the hunt works.

This is where the concept of intrapreneurship comes in. The first time I heard that word, it was from the entrepreneur-in-residence at the University of Louisville during a tech visit to Indianapolis. Honestly, I was offended. I felt like someone was hijacking the identity I'd bled to become. But in hindsight, they were right.

Great teams are built with intrapreneurs. People who think like owners. People who take risks, create solutions, and raise their hand even when no one asks. It's a trait I look for in everyone I hire.

When we built our latest SaaS platform, I was gone for ten days. The team executed 90% of the build while I was out—and they improved on my original concept. That's intrapreneurship in action.

Even if you're not the founder, you can be number six, seven, or eight on a rocket ship—and end up with a massive piece of the upside.

You eat what you kill. And sometimes, what you build.

## The Importance of Health, Fitness, and Mental Clarity

You are the weapon.

The emails, the ads, the funnels, the sales calls—those are just arrows in your quiver. But you are the one who draws the bow.

That's why your health matters. That's why your energy matters. That's why your mental clarity is not optional.

Fitness isn't vanity. It's vitality. Sleep isn't weakness. It's a weapon. Meditation isn't woo-woo. It's tuning your signal so you can hear your own damn thoughts.

The entrepreneur who takes care of their body and mind has an unfair advantage. You make better decisions. You regulate stress. You outlast your competitors, not because you're smarter, but because you're sharper.

Every decision, every pitch, every pivot comes from your internal ecosystem. Protect it. Optimize it. Worship it, even.

Because the hunter doesn't get a second shot.

## How to Sustain Motivation for the Long Haul

Let me break it to you gently: you're going to want to quit.

And like way more than just once.

There will be days when nothing clicks. When the leads dry up. When the team disappoints. When your bank account talks back.

Motivation won't save you. But rhythm will.

You build these systems not because you're soft—but because you're going to be tested.

I want you to picture a moment. It's March 2020. You flip on the news—lockdowns. Closures. Panic. Your phone is blowing up. Clients are pulling back. Friends are scared. The world is unraveling at the seams.

I remember standing in my living room, lights off, eyes glued to the blue glow of the TV. The world felt frozen. People were hoarding toilet paper. Businesses were closing by the hour. Governors were issuing mandates. One day to the next, you didn't know if your income was safe or your family was in danger.

That wasn't a stress test. That was a war game.

I was living in Louisville, Kentucky—ground zero for a nation on edge. The Breonna Taylor riots were igniting downtown, just blocks from people I love. Helicopters circled the skyline. Sirens never stopped. Armed National Guard troops stood on street corners like it was Baghdad, not the Bluegrass State. Grocery store shelves were bare. People whispered about martial law. Curfews were in place. The air smelled like tension and tear gas.

And in the midst of that, I had businesses to run. A family to feed. A mission to lead. It felt like fucking World War III.

This was more than a political debate or a temporary disruption. It was a line-in-the-sand moment. Would you retreat—or rise? Would you freeze—or fight?

And here's the thing: no one was coming to save you. Not the government. Not your landlord. Not your employer. The people who made it through had systems. They had fallback plans. They had conviction.

I had built routines that kept me moving even when the world told me to sit still. When they told me to put a mask on, I said no. When they told me to close my doors, I kept them open. When they told me to stop hugging my parents, I wrapped my arms tighter.

Not because I'm rebellious. Okay— maybe I am— a little. But because I know this truth: in a world that can flip overnight, discipline is not optional.

You don't rise to the occasion—you fall to the level of your preparation.

So don't rely on inspiration. Build systems that run even when you don't feel like showing up. Create routines that carry you when your legs are tired. Anchor to rituals that remind you who you are.

Because with liberty comes responsibility. And with responsibility comes power.

That's what our Founders understood. That's what the modern hunter lives by.

## Battle-Tested Challenge: What Will You Do When the World Shifts Again?

You've now seen what happens when the world pulls the rug out from under you. It's not a question of if it will happen again—it's when.

Will you scramble, or will you already be in motion? Will you fold, or will your habits hold? Will you ask permission to act, or will you move like your life depends on it—because in a way, it does?

The modern hunter isn't built on vibes. He's built on vision. He doesn't flinch at chaos—he was born in it.

Your job now is to build a life so stable, so grounded in systems, rhythm, health, and ownership... that no storm can stop your hunt.

# CHAPTER 10

# Ascending to Apex: Becoming the Ultimate Entrepreneur

## The Call Before the Crown

*Before the world knew crowns, there were callings.*
*Before there were kings, there were hearts set ablaze.*
*In the hidden places—where fire burns hottest and the herd fears to tread—there stands a throne, not carved by craftsmen, but forged in trial and revealed by grace.*
*Bone by bone. Scar by scar.*

*Every fragment a lesson. Every fracture a prayer answered.*
*This is not the seat of the proud; it is the seat of the prepared.*
*Men cannot crown what God has already called.*
*Ask—not for riches, but for wisdom—and Heaven will pour it out without measure.*
*The throne was once a metaphor; now it is a mandate: dominion is born of divine alignment.*

*If your spirit stirs at this sight, remember you were born to hunt, to build, to rise.*

*Rise, son of fire. Step forward, daughter of grit.*

*The Throne of Bones awaits those who walk in wisdom and lead with holy fire in their chests.*

# The Final Evolution: From Hunter to Apex

If these words reach you, you have endured the furnace. You have hunted, fought, stumbled, and bled. You have claimed momentum, sharpened skill, and tasted ownership. But this chapter is no longer about what you *do*. It is about who you are *becoming*.

Most never arrive here. They quit in the valley, drift in the wilderness, or settle once the fridge is full and the bills are paid. Not you. The Apex Predator presses on—not from greed but from revelation: you were not made to survive; you were forged to dominate.

The Apex is measured by alignment, not trophies. It is the collision of gift and tested character, of resilience and refined skill. Here purpose becomes power and leadership becomes legacy.

You are no longer chasing. You are now carrying. You built the throne; now you must rule from it.

> *"I hated every minute of training, but I said, 'Don't quit. Suffer now and live the rest of your life as a champion.'"* — Muhammad Ali, Louisville's own.

Ali's crown was not talent; it was tenacity. When the fire dimmed, he trained anyway. When the world pressed him down, he stood taller. That is the spirit of the Apex.

Consider also my friend Ryan Stewman. From rock-bottom arrests to a multi-million-dollar empire, he proves that excuses are chains. His creed is simple:

*No coach, partner, parent, or politician is coming. Decide to wage war on the gap between your potential and your performance.*

His "Apex" movement echoes every lesson of this book: discipline over drama, clarity over comfort, execution over emotion.

The throne of bones is not a monument to suffering; it is a memorial to ownership.

# The Apex Code — Your Final Framework

Hype has served its purpose; clarity must carry you the rest of the way. Success can soften a hunter faster than failure ever could. The Apex Code keeps the edge keen.

I have worn it down to four letters: **A.P.E.X.**

## A — Adapt

The wild crowns the adaptable. Seasons shift, algorithms change, buyers evolve. When a strategy breaks, do not panic or blame—*pivot with power and hunt again.*

## P — Persist

Adaptation keeps you alive; persistence makes you legendary. Betrayal, downturns, doubts—bleed forward anyway. Anchor into purpose and press on. God promised strength, not ease.

## E — Execute

Talk feeds no family. Vision boards build no empires. Pull the trigger. Make the call. Post the video. Execution births data, data sharpens strategy, strategy funds freedom.

## X — X-Factor

You cannot fake it or force it. The X-Factor is your divine fingerprint on the marketplace—where gift, grit, and obedience converge. You become magnetic, not because you are loud, but because you are *anchored*.

> **A.P.E.X.**: Adapt when others freeze. Persist when others fold. Execute when others delay. Activate the X-Factor only you carry.

This is not a tactic; it is a transformation.

# Refocus Your *Why* — The Last Real Test

At the summit, comfort, not competition, destroys most men. Hunger without purpose mutates into ego; power without love into tyranny. Return to the sacred ground of the heart. Love is not weakness—it is the assignment.

Napoleon Hill's *Outwitting the Devil* warns that drifting begins the moment a man forgets his definite purpose. Distraction is destruction in disguise.

*You are not drifting; you are driven.*

Pause. Breathe. Listen for the whisper beneath the roar. Let it realign you. If purpose is clear and the heart is open, nothing—*nothing*—can stop you.

Now rise. The throne is waiting.

**Action Step:** Take 30 minutes today to audit your life through the lens of A.P.E.X. Identify one concrete action for each letter that you will execute in the next seven days. Document it, commit to it, and refuse to let comfort invade.

*The spear will never hit the ground again.*

# EPILOGUE

# Licking Your Lips – The Path Forward

You made it.

If you're still here—pages deep, blood in your teeth, heart on fire—then you're not just a reader. You're a hunter now. You've seen the terrain. You've faced the internal war. You've stood at the edge of the wild and decided not to turn back.

But before we part ways, let's take a breath. Let's sharpen the blade one more time. Let's lock in the lessons, forge the next steps, and walk into the future *dangerous and deliberate.*

## Reviewing the Lessons Learned

This wasn't just a mindset book. It was a map. And don't forget to get all the expanded content, drawings and frame works absolutely free at [TheHunterHeadGame.com](TheHunterHeadGame.com)

You've learned what it means to shift from the hunted to the hunter—to stop reacting and start *relentlessly pursuing*.

You've built confidence by confronting your fears, replacing hesitation with action.

You've embraced discomfort, discipline, and the predator's pace.

You discovered what it means to build your own *Throne of Bones*—piece by piece, lesson by lesson.

You learned how to track, plan, strike, and lead.

And maybe most importantly, you learned the truth no one talks about. That this isn't just business—it's *spiritual.*

Because when you're walking in alignment with God's purpose, your moves carry eternal weight.

## Creating Your Personalized Action Plan

This isn't a feel-good story. It's a call to *move*. So, here's your moment of reflection—your kill plan.

First, ask yourself:

- What's one hunt I've been *avoiding*?
- Where am I still *drifting* or *contemplating*?
- What should I be *deciding*?
- What tool(s) do I need to *sharpen* next to achieve my goals?

Write it down. Put it in your calendar. Put it on your mirror. Etch it into your mind like a war cry.

You've done the internal work. Now, it's time for deliberate, aligned execution. Don't just chase goals—hunt them with obsession. Don't just build wealth—build *impact*.

And don't forget: *The spear doesn't throw itself.* You must be the one to move first.

## The Commitment to Lifelong Learning and Growth

The Apex Predator never retires. He evolves. He expands. He deepens. You don't reach the top and sit still—you keep your blade sharp through curiosity, humility, and commitment to growth.

Read more. Learn from mentors. Train your body. Strengthen your mind. Quiet your soul. Talk to God.

Every single day is another rep.

The hunters who last?

They're the ones who stay students, no matter how big the game gets.

## Now, It's Time to Hunt

This is not where the fire ends. It's where it *ignites everything else in your life.*

You have a framework.
You have the mindset.
You have the calling.

You've come face-to-face with the throne. You've remembered your why. You've tasted what it means to walk in purpose.

Now, it's time to *take everything you've learned... and go hunt something bigger.*

> *Do not return to the village empty-handed.*
> *Do not shrink now that you've been stretched.*
> *Do not forget who you are when the world tries to tame you.*

The jungle is waiting.

And so is your legacy.

Go sharpen your teeth.

Go raise your spear.

It's time to hunt.

## Final Words.

This book was over ten years in the making.

Not just in writing...
but in living. In failing. In rebuilding. In learning how to hunt again with intention, with faith, and with fire.

And if you've made it to this page—
I want you to know something most people never hear:

I'm proud of you.

I'm proud of you for picking up a book with a title as bold and raw as *The Hunter Head Game*.

I'm proud of you for not just flipping a few pages and setting it down like most do.

For leaning in.
For staying with it.
For staying with *yourself*.

Most people never make it past Chapter One.
Most people avoid the mirror.
Most people get uncomfortable and turn back.

But you?
You stayed.
You sharpened your spear.
You faced the shadows.
You listened when your heart whispered that there had to be *more*.

You leaned into your higher calling—
Not just for you, but for your family, your team, your legacy...
your *assignment*.

And if no one has told you this in a while:

You are not average.
You are not late.
You are not lost.

You were just waiting to be *called*.

And now you've heard the call.

So go lead.
Go hunt.
Go *build something unshakable*.
The kind of life only a dangerous, aligned, God-anchored Apex could build.

The jungle will not get easier.

But now...
you're ready.

— Coach Carroll

# The Apex Hunter: Battle Plan

*Sign it in ink. Live it in blood.*

**1. My Next Hunt:**
*What is the mission I must pursue now without excuse or delay?*

_____

_____


**2. Weapons I Must Sharpen:**
*What skill, tool, or mindset must be upgraded immediately?*

_____

_____


**3. My Apex Non-Negotiables:**
*These are the lines I will no longer cross, compromise, or delay.*

_____

_____

**4. My X-Factor Commitments:**
*How will I lead with love, purpose, and divine alignment?*

_____

_____


**5. My Words to Myself (when things get hard):**
*Write a message from your Apex self to your future self for when you feel weak.*

_____

_____


**Signature:**

_____

**Date:**

_____

*You are not the hunted. You are the hunter.*
*The throne is yours now. Go feed your legacy.*

# References

Cardone, Grant. *The 10X Rule: The Only Difference Between Success and Failure*. Wiley, 2011.

Fenton, Richard, and Andrea Waltz. *Go for No! Yes Is the Destination, No Is How You Get There*. Courage Crafters Inc., 2007.

Gitomer, Jeffrey. *The Little Red Book of Selling: 12.5 Principles of Sales Greatness*. Bard Press, 2004.

Hill, Napoleon. *Outwitting the Devil: The Secret to Freedom and Success*. Sterling, 2011.

Martell, Dan. *Buy Back Your Time: Get Unstuck, Reclaim Your Freedom, and Build Your Empire*. Portfolio, 2023.

Robbins, Tony. Referenced for teachings on the "Law of Association."

Rohn, Jim. Referenced for his teachings on the "Law of Association" and how we are the average of the five people we spend the most time with.

Stewman, Ryan. *Apex* and "No Excuses" mentality references from Ryan Stewman's teachings and programs.

Tadevosyan, Hayk. Referenced for insights on referral strategies in business.

Vaynerchuk, Gary. Concept of "macro patience, micro speed" referenced in business philosophy.

Voss, Chris, and Tahl Raz. *Never Split the Difference: Negotiating As If Your Life Depended On It*. Harper Business, 2016.

Willink, Jocko, and Leif Babin. *Extreme Ownership: How U.S. Navy SEALs Lead and Win*. St. Martin's Press, 2015.

Ziglar, Zig. Referenced for teachings on the "Law of Association."

www.ingramcontent.com/pod-product-compliance
Lightning Source LLC
Chambersburg PA
CBHW040236110526
44582CB00021B/207/J